AND SHE THINKS
WE'RE JUST RACING!

BY TROY DANA

And She Thinks We're Just Racing!

INTERESTED IN SPONSORING JESSICA DANA?

Jessica Dana Racing is a small team of family and friends who joined together to support Jessica's big dreams.

Combined with raw talent, Jessica quickly learns and applies new information, and she is dedicated to doing whatever it takes to improve her racecraft.

Running a limited schedule in 2011 due to funding constraints, Jessica finished half her races in the top-5.

With additional sponsorship, the sky's the limit for Jessica Dana.

If you are interested in becoming a sponsor and helping Jessica attain her racing dreams, contact Troy Dana at Troy.Dana@d3rec.com

FOR THE LATEST NEWS ON JESSICA DANA

Visit www.JessicaDanaRacing.com.

CONTENTS

INTRODUCTION — AND SHE THINKS WE'RE JUST RACING

"An optimist is someone who will go after Moby Dick in a row boat and take tartar sauce" — Zig Ziglar

The initial intent of the book was to write about a talented little girl, my little girl, and her Dad, and the amazingly close relationship and adventures they shared while preparing her for life and imparting words of wisdom until one day she grows up, gets married and the story comes to an end.

In reality this book is about me and the life lessons my daughter has taught and shared with me. In an odd and remarkably delightful way, my daughter has in her own way reminded me of these words of wisdom and thoughtful encouragement I said to her each and every time we went to a race in the early days: "You could be and do anything if your heart and mind are there at that moment."

For this story to be told properly it is important to capture my childhood experiences and lessons learned, and how those have influenced me both as a father and husband. If occasionally as you read the early chapters of this book you find yourself saying "run, Forrest, run," you're not alone!

Each and every new experience and adventure I shared with my daughter Jessica brought to me the most amazing pride, joy and peace I have ever known in my life. Racing was never the plan; initially it was just another chance for me to spend time with my daughter in another adventure of sorts, in this case an indoor go-kart facility near our home. It was a safe and dry environment — being lifelong residents of Washington State that's a consideration! — close to our house and it was a ton of fun. Two years later almost to the day what started out as an amusement park go-kart ride evolved into more than an opportunity for Jessica, it very well may shape her future.

1

But racing with Jessica has given me, her father (I still prefer Daddy), and dozens and dozens of friends and family an experience impossible to put into words. And she still thinks we're just racing.

As a father, I like all fathers wanted my little girl to feel safe, I wanted her to never question if she was loved and I wanted her to be confident that she could truly do anything she wanted if she was dedicated and determined. This is the typical inspirational speech given by every loving father who expects those words of wisdom to sink in but is still shocked when the child executes on the message.

At no point did I ever expect or want anything more than her happiness and for her to enjoy life. This goal was made simple in so far as I was blessed to have married the most wonderful woman in my wife Pam, whose close and loving relationship with her father Mel is something I instantly saw and admired. They enjoy a wonderful father-daughter bond and I am sure he cherishes his relationship with Pam (his daughter) as much today as my wife and I do with Jessica.

My father-in-law is all about family first; his leadership, integrity and values make Mel one of the great men I have known and who have influenced me. Most importantly, I learned from him you can still enjoy a loving and kind relationship with your children years after they embark on their own journey. Mel's patriarchal qualities have given me the confidence and courage to know parenting involves more than holding the title and parenting with fear and intimidation. My wife's father is an inspiration and a role model for me and my wife as well as the entire family.

This amazing man also had a profoundly positive influence on my daughter's life because he too encouraged his children as well as his grandchildren to challenge themselves and to be great when it's your time to be great. I do however believe to this day racing was the last thing he had in mind. Words will never express how much respect, admiration and love I have for Mel.

In addition I have to acknowledge my own father. While it could be argued he was not always a perfect father, he truly loved his children and wanted each of his three kids to be the best they could be.

This book is first dedicated to my daughter Jessica for without her my life today would have no purpose, my wife who is my inspiration and soul mate, my father for being tough on me day-in and day-out, and my entire family. While I may not show it or express it well I love you all more then you could ever know.

CHAPTER 1 — IT'S NOT ABOUT ME ... REALLY!

On a warm summer day in 1967 or '68, the floral scent of flowers and lilac trees was in the still thick warm air of West Seattle. The sun was warm on our faces and exposed skin as my little brother and I sat on the lawn about to eat our lunch.

Several yellow jackets were buzzing about after having zeroed in on our PB&Js and Kool-Aid, but we were having a picnic. Yes, a picnic in the backyard of the place we called our home at the time, a tiny new house we'd lived in for three or four days on Genesee Hill. We had a blanket on the ground, there was obviously food and drink but something was missing.

We were by ourselves, 3, 4 or maybe 5 years old, my little brother and me. Mom was nowhere to be found and Dad was at work.

Mom had been there to get us set up to have the picnic, but now here we were alone, 50 feet from the steps leading into the back porch of the dark blue two-bedroom, one-bath rambler. My brother and I sat alone on the slightly over-grown, weedy, and tacky to the touch grass having a picnic with the bees, bugs and ants as our guests. I think we were having a good time, but I'm just not sure because I don't think we had ever had a picnic before. But at that moment, when I suppose we were having a good time, the unthinkable happened.

An ear-piercing wail shattered the peaceful sounds of life in our little community, instantly changing our backyard from a safe and secure environment to one filled with sheer terror. It was loud, like nothing we had heard in our short lives, and it was a most terrifying moment for two young children to face with no adult nearby.

The sound came from a siren and looking back now I realize it could have been some sort of early warning system being tested at that time. As my little brother and I ran screaming to the house to get inside, where it was safe and Mom could give us protection, we found something that made the situation much worse: The door was locked; we could not get in.

Our terror escalated and now we began kicking and pounding on the door, screaming at the top of our lungs. After what seemed like an eternity, Mom — with frustration etched on her face — unlocked the door and shoved us in the house where we needed a few minutes to calm down. This angry look we saw in her face many times growing up.

To this day I have no idea why we were locked out but I am sure there was a good reason for it.

As summer came to an end I knew my world would change because now I had to go to school. I was not prepared however for getting beat with the belt for several hours for not be able to tie my shoes the night before my first day of school. I wondered if all the kids had bruises all over their butts on the first day. I was too young to know any better at that time, but I learned at an early age my learning curve was likely going to include lots whippings with the belt.

Not long after the first day of school I started to realize all of the friends I had in the neighborhood called their parents "Mommy" and "Daddy." One day, I made the mistake of calling my father "Daddy" in front of my friend Mike, who lived behind our house. My Dad corrected me quickly and firmly: "real" men don't say Mommy and Daddy, they say Mom and Dad. There it was at 5 years old: my brother and I had a Mom and a Dad, we were not to say Mommy or Daddy.

Now I am sure my parents were very affectionate with us before we were 4 or 5, but until I turned 17 I do not remember my parents telling either my brother or I that they loved us, snuggling with us or doing anything that resembled outward affection. If we were scared at night and could not sleep, we were required to deal with it: we were not allowed to crawl in bed with Mom and Dad. I recall crying myself to sleep many times as a child, feeling scared or disconnected from my parents.

Not that I am making excuses, they took good care of us and compared to their own childhoods this was a cake walk for me and my brother. I later learned I did not have what many would consider model parents. My mother had dropped out of high school in ninth grade and she was just 16 when I was born. My father dropped out in tenth grade; he was 18 or 19 at my birth.

Both came from homes of absolute poverty and the parents on both sides were divorced. Add to this cocktail the fact that both had very odd and mostly dysfunctional relationships with one or both sets of my grandparents and it is a wonder they were able to accomplish what they did.

Things were different in those days. It was not uncommon to have children at a younger age and marry at an age society would consider young by today's standards, but they chose to take a more challenging path in life by marrying to get away from their reality at that time. I give them all the credit in the world because in their own way they tried to give my brother and I the childhood they never had. At times we truly had a wonderful childhood: we went to Disneyland a couple times, and we had the same bikes, toys and games most all the other kids had. I am convinced these experiences, together with the influence of the best friend I would meet some years down the road and one more added twist, influenced me in every way.

That added twist would be the common occurrence of hearing the words: "Guess what? We're moving." More about that later, but I came to know those sentences all too well over the years.

CHAPTER 2 — MINI-BIKE DREAMS TO MOTORCYCLE REALITY

The year I finished first grade we were still living in West Seattle. My Dad was working as a diesel mechanic on boats in Lake Union, downtown Seattle, and my Mom had a job at JC Penny selling shoes.

With school finishing up and summer just around the corner, I began to ask my Dad about getting a mini-bike. Several boys in the neighborhood ran their Honda mini-bikes up and down the pothole-filled gravel alley — often soaked in used motor oil to keep the dust down — behind our little house, and I thought they looked like so much fun with their big round tires and loud, smelly engines. I desperately wanted to have one.

By this time I was a pretty good bicycle rider for a 6 year old and I shared a love for riding on two wheels with my Dad, who had been thinking about taking up off-road motorcycle riding. Occasionally Dad would take me to the local motorcycle shop where, like any young boy seeing all the brand-new motorcycles lined up smallest to largest, I would dream of someday having one of my own.

One day Dad announced he had purchased a Kawasaki 175; it was the coolest thing I ever saw. Now that I could touch, feel and smell a real motorcycle I knew I had to have one of my own someday. But right then I wanted a mini-bike so I could go ride with my Dad.

Dad and his best friend Terry had each bought the exact same bike and would ride together whenever they could. Every time they pulled out of the driveway and left me behind I felt like I didn't belong; it was torture not to be with them. I dreamed of the day I would get a mini-bike and spent a lot of time thinking about what it would be like to ride. The wide tires, thick padded seat and entry-level design would make riding it easy for me, but I was also a little fearful of how difficult it might prove to control one of these cool machines.

In theory my assessment was correct: with no shifting and no clutch, just a throttle and brake, a mini-bike would be a very safe first step for a 6 year old to get started on the path to riding motorcycles, especially a smaller rider.

Now that my Dad and his buddy Terry had bikes, I wanted a mini-bike more than ever. So badly did I want it that I began to obsess about getting one. With handle bars made from tree branches and using my lips to make motor sounds — *vroom, vroom, VROOM!* — I would run around the backyard pretending to ride my very own mini-bike. I wanted one so bad I likely badgered my Dad with it day after day.

It seemed like forever, but six months after he got his bike my Dad told me to get in the truck. It was a red, short-bed half-ton GMC pickup with dual exhaust and a three-speed transmission with a granny gear — that truck sounded so cool. Dad and I drove to the motorcycle shop where he got his bike but there was not a great deal of bikes my size, so we drove to the Yamaha shop in Federal Way and there it was: a Yamaha 60 Enduro motorcycle!

The Enduro was perfect for me, except it had skinny tires and a clutch and gears, four of them. But, darn it, it had skinny tires; I could never ride this thing! I was scared and tried to plead with my Dad, telling him I wanted the fat tires, low seat and no gears of a mini-bike. After I said "Dad, I can't ride this thing," he told me in his very fatherly and kind, gentle way: "You will figure out how to ride this bike or you won't ride anything." He continued, telling me the Yamaha 60 was a real bike, not a sissy mini-bike, and it was the only two-wheel option on the table. Otherwise, "You can just ride your bicycle and the men will ride motorcycles."

Of course I took the Yamaha. I was scared but determined to figure it out so I could go with him and not be left at home.

We had no garage and no storage area at our tiny house in West Seattle, so we kept our motorcycles in a rust-streaked steel shipping container my Dad found. In our neighborhood, things disappeared frequently if they were not locked up or chained down. My new motorcycle sat in the shipping container, out of my reach and inaccessible, for what seemed like forever before Dad was willing to spend some time teaching me to ride. Finally — I am sure it was not more than a week or two that passed, perhaps just a few days — Dad was ready to let me try riding my bike. As was his custom, Dad drank a number of beers before the lesson, so my first riding experience was memorable for more than one reason.

On this particular day my father was not particularly patient or calm while teaching me how to ride: "Here put this helmet on ... This is the brake, this is gear shift, this is the clutch and this is how you start it." Although he showed me how to kick start the bike, I couldn't do it. Barely reaching the ground on my tippy-toes — it was clear even then I was not going to be very tall; in every class picture there I was, a first-row short kid — I kicked and kicked with all my little 6 year old leg had to give, but it didn't work.

Dad was instantly frustrated, but he started the bike for me.

After my 10 second education on the fine art of letting the clutch out without killing the motor and giving it gas, he said assertively: "Ride!" I was afraid, but he pushed the bike with me on it, his hand on the back bar holding me up. I looked back to make sure he was holding the bike up for me while he yelled commands: "Let the clutch out," "Give it a little gas." And what do you know, I could ride the bike confidently, knowing he was holding onto the back bar for me!

I started off slow, too slow, and the bike was about to die so he said "GIVE IT SOME GAS" so loud I thought he was yelling at me, so I did! I twisted the grip and the engine roared to life, I guess I probably got the bike moving at about 18 miles per hour but unfortunately Dad was only good to about 15 and he took a wicked tumble right there in the alley. Dad spent the next couple of weeks pulling gravel out of his hands and elbows —and wow, did he bleed a lot — but fortunately for me by that time he had drank enough beer that I don't think he felt it all that much. Lucky for me, because a miscue like that was usually good for three of four swats with the belt.

I was basically on my own after that first 15-minute lesson. Dad was not about to hold the back bar anymore but I still had the urge to ride up and down the alley, or in the backyard or on the street; it did not matter as long as I could ride. A couple more trips down and back in the alley and Dad told me to park it because he needed to wash the blood off his hands and arms.

My first riding experience was over. I had poor throttle control, as I had learned when I stretched his right arm out six feet just before he hit the ground, but Dad said I was ready enough to ride without him holding me up or helping let the clutch out — so surely I must have been.

CHAPTER 3 — FIRST RIDE AWAY FROM HOME

It could have been a month, it could have been several months — I am not sure, funny how time works in your memories — but sometime after my first riding experience in the alley Dad said we were going to ride bikes with Terry. Terry was a slender, kind-hearted neighbor who over the years became my Dad's best friend.

Dad loaded our bikes in the red GMC pickup with dual exhaust and we drove to a gravel pit area near Kent, Washington, as I recall, with our motorcycles tied down with heavy yellow nylon ropes in the back of the truck. Loading and tying the bikes down was an ordeal I had just learned but I didn't care: I was so excited just to be in the truck with my Dad that I nearly peed in my pants when we pulled into the parking area. Terry pulled in and parked right beside us with his brand new Kawasaki 175, which was the identical twin of my Dad's brand new Kawasaki 175. There I was getting ready for my first ride and I had no clue what I was supposed to do or what was expected of me, but I was so excited to be riding with my Dad that I didn't care.

As we pulled to a stop and got out of the truck, I was intimidated by what I saw. The gravel pit was a huge riding area, with piles of dirt, hills, trails and jumps. Panic set in: I needed flat ground, I needed the alley with potholes and nothing more!

Dad and Terry decided they should hydrate before riding, so each drank a beer or two. This was customary, I later learned, before and during every recreational riding event. As for me, the second my bike was on the ground I was sitting on it, pretending to be riding and looking cool. That earned a quick bark from Dad, who told me to get off the bike so he could check things and then start it. He pulled out the kick starter and kicked it over a few times, yelling at me to pay attention.

"Here's the choke," he said. "Once it starts turn the choke off — got it?" With a couple of swift kicks, *vroom*, the motor came to life. Once it had warmed up a little, he revved up the tiny motor, I guess to show Terry and I how many revs it could do. Once it was properly warmed up, Dad told me to put my "hat" on, code for helmet, and to ride "right over there" where he and Terry could watch me, "and don't go anywhere else."

I was so proud of myself, driving in circles in first gear, going around to the right then to the left, as I became more confident in my riding skills. I kept looking around to see if my Dad was watching and sure enough there he was with a watchful eye on me. Another glance and I noticed Dad and Terry getting ready to go for a ride; a few moments later I crashed. Nothing serious but just enough to learn I was too small to pick the bike up on my own and I still was not ready to start it. Dad came over, picked me up and started the bike again; I could not even begin to lift that thing up. He told me the next time I crashed I would either pick it up myself or I wouldn't ride, so I tried harder not to crash!

This was pretty cool, Dad and Terry drank more beer and I rode around in circles. But at the point that I was getting braver and more interested in showing off all my acquired skills as a rider, I noticed my Dad and Terry had left the truck with their bikes. They were gone and I had no idea where they were, if it was my own fault for going where I shouldn't have or if they were out looking for me. Being caught up in the moment of just learning to ride and the freedom that came with it, I had not been paying attention to what was going on around me.

Feeling a little frightened and lost, I wandered away from the truck on my bike, being sure to stay on flat ground as I was not at all ready to cope with varied topography. Even though I was uneasy about getting too far away from the truck, I kept riding because boy, did I love it. It was less scary and more enticing the faster I rode, so I shifted up to second and then third gear. I was going faster and having more fun but a key piece of my learning how to ride was missing.

Dad must have forgotten to tell me about slowing down or downshifting, and when these little bits of information would have been most useful I had no idea what to do. I just narrowly missed hitting a man on a big motorcycle, and I was going so fast I was afraid to do anything but close my eyes and hold tight as all my 6 years of life experience told me I was about to hit something hard. I'm not sure how, but I stayed upright and was able to kill the engine after the near miss with the brakes.

And oh, no, the man on the big bike stopped, looking back at me with anger on his face as I had nearly wrecked us both. He turned around and rode up to park next to me. Thinking he was pretty pissed off, I was scared to death; I looked around for Dad and Terry but they were still nowhere to be seen. The man I almost wrecked asked me if I was okay and where my Dad was. When I told him I didn't know, he asked where we were parked and I was able to point to our truck. He started my bike for me and together we rode back to the truck, and then the man told me firmly to stay put until my Dad got back.

It was not long before Dad and Terry came back, and as they each opened another beer and began talking about their ride and asking where I had rode off to, Dad said firmly "I told you to stay here where I could see you." The man who I nearly wrecked came over to talk to Dad a few minutes later, and figuring I was in real trouble I hid around the front of the truck. I was so accustomed to getting beaten with his belt for doing things wrong or being bad that I expected more of the same for this, but oddly that wasn't the case this time. Dad told me to get my head out of my ass and I could get hurt if I did not pay attention, and then he and Terry proceeded to tell me how dangerous riding was and how it was important to use good judgment or something like that. They hydrated with another beer and then went for another ride before we loaded the bikes and went home.

As parents go my Dad was Superman in my eyes and I always wanted him to be proud of me. By contrast my father's Dad, Grandpa Bill, was not much of a role model or father to my Dad. This is just my opinion but all accounts of his life, the ones I heard about or saw, gave me the feeling he was a cowardly braggart and alcoholic with no interest in his family, kids or community; his only interest was himself. He left my grandmother with four kids to care for while living in a small house with sawdust floors and never gave her any support except for the occasional offer to buy dinner for the kids on payday. On the rare occasion my family would travel to visit Grandpa

Bill, he would tell us stories about all his fist fights and logging lore, and how he was the best equipment operator in the state, maybe the country. My Dad would often tell me stories about his relationship with his father and once I was old enough to understand more, I realized a few beatings now and then with the belt was a cake walk. What my Dad went through with his father made my childhood feel like Disneyland by comparison.

One day Dad came home to our tiny West Seattle house and announced we would be moving to a nice new house near an old vacant Weyerhaeuser property in Federal Way where hundreds of people rode motorcycles every day. The new house had an amazing tree fort, a carport with an area where we could securely store our motorcycles and bicycles, and best of all it was close enough to a riding area at that time known to us as the Federal Way Riding Pit. He told us how much we would enjoy our new school and would enjoy being so close to the riding area. We would ride all the time and maybe someday I would get to start racing motorcycles. I was so excited I started packing my toys and stuff — I was ready to move that day — because my Dad could paint an amazing picture of how life would be.

On my last day of school in West Seattle, however, I was overwhelmed with emotions I did not understand as I got my first experience saying goodbye to friends and leaving the safety and comfort of belonging. This turned out to be something I've never fully learned how to deal with or control, the emotion that comes with never feeling like I belonged. This would become a reoccurring theme in my life and it clearly influenced my values when it came to children in general and more specifically, my child.

CHAPTER 4 — READY TO RACE

We moved to Federal Way, Washington and my new school was Lake Grove Elementary; it was a great school but I missed my friends from West Seattle. It was not easy for me to connect with kids but I did become good friends with Mark who lived across the street and a couple others who lived nearby.

Much to my disappointment we did not get to ride motorcycles at the vacant Weyerhaeuser Pit site just south of Federal Way as promised, even though we lived just three miles away. We met plenty of new kids who shared a passion for riding bicycles and found lots of fun places to ride them, but as for riding motorcycles at the greatest place I knew of at that time, the Federal Way trails, it was just not important to my Dad. He would often tell me we would go there, but pretty soon I realized that just was not the case. I don't recall for sure but I think in the two years we lived in Federal Way we made it to the greatest riding place known to me twice.

A couple years passed with me riding once every few months and making one trip to the Cle Elum Coal Piles in Eastern Washington; I had so much fun there! Then Dad started talking about taking me to a real racetrack, Jolly Rodgers. He told me I was becoming a very good rider and with him working on my bike to provide the horsepower — as a diesel mechanic, Dad said he could give me more horses than anyone else — I should be able to beat every other kid out there. If he said it, I believed it!

This was also about the time my father began teaching me the value of being tough. Nine-year-old boys would fight from time to time, and he said if I was not going to be the toughest kid in school I needed to at least be one of the toughest. In his best fatherly way, Dad wanted me to be okay and to hold my own, so whenever he felt it was needed Dad would remind me to stand up to bullies and to protect myself and my brother. He told me to make it known that no one should mess with me, and his suggested way of making that happen was for me to take on the toughest bully in school and simply kick his ass. Once I did that, no one would ever pick on me again.

Regrettably, as the shortest and one of the smallest kids in class this did not turn out to be very good advice. But, at 9 I was armed with a new attitude and confidence. Perhaps I didn't know any better, but at any rate I was ready to take on any challenge because Dad said that is what I needed to do.

I learned quickly Dusty was the kid I needed to teach a lesson. Dusty was scary: he was much bigger than all the kids our age and he relished being the tough guy. His father encouraged this arrogant attitude and all the kids in the neighborhood knew Dusty was one bad ass; no one liked him, either. One day Dusty was doing his usual bullying so I hit him square in the face with a block of ice. Dusty never picked on me again but my Dad beat me with the belt for using a block of ice to hit Dusty after Dusty's father complained to Dad it was not a fair fight. Throughout my school career I batted .500 — winning about as many fights as I lost — when it came to taking on the biggest, toughest guy in school. That actually helped my confidence and allowed me to compete and be more aggressive on an even playing field, so I thank my Dad for all the trophies, but I'm not sure how much I enjoyed getting beat up half the time.

Before I took on Dusty, Dad decided I would enter my first real race at Jolly Rogers at the ripe old age of 8. On race day we loaded up my bike, helmet and what riding gear we had at the time, and I was as anxious as anyone would be before their first competition. Of course I did not know what to expect but I thought I would be racing against kids my own age. Little did I know my competition would be a lineup of 10-, 11- and 12-year-old kids.

The day was a typical cold, rainy winter day in the Pacific Northwest, but that fact did not matter: I was at a real motorcycle track with my Dad and I was confident because he was there. Dad gave me the rundown as he helped me line up in the pits: You are going to have some practice laps to get familiar with the track, do you know what a green flag means? How about white flag? Checkered flag?

He told me to start in first gear but got impatient when he could see I had no idea what he was trying to communicate to me. Frustrated, he said "Rev the motor and then give it full throttle right after letting out the clutch when you see the green flag drop. You have to race these guys into the first corner," he continued, "When you come out of the first corner shift down and you will blow by everyone. Make sure you don't use too much rear brake or you will skid; use too much front brake and you will crash." He was communicating to me as if I was going to be competitive on day one!

That was the half-minute download just before my first race. For an 8-year old boy, it was like drinking from a fire hose.

After a few practice laps and a drivers meeting to explain the flags and race rules, my class was called to the starting line, which Dad had to point me in the direction of. I lined up, ready for my first race, but when the green flag dropped there I sat, motor revved up to maximum RPM. Oops, not in gear. I saw Dad across the track waving franticly to *GO!*, so I kicked the shift lever down and gunned the motor — not even sure if I was going the right way. Before even getting to the first turn I had shifted into second and then third gear, not knowing exactly what I was expected to do.

Kids from 8 to 12 all racing similar bikes in the same class doesn't seem like much of a difference to someone who is 25, but at that time it was a huge disadvantage. Dad was not a good cheerleader nor was he altogether very inspiring, but I knew I would be okay, that he should be proud if I could manage to finish the race. Every lap that I passed him I would look at Dad to see if he was watching me and it was just luck I didn't crash right in front of him — or maybe I did crash right in front of him.

Every lap of the race I would glance over to see if he was watching me but after the third or fourth time around I saw him with a beer in his hand, talking to someone parked next to us. I suspect he was bored watching me run dead last.

I don't recall how many races we entered where I ran proficiently and competently in the back of the pack, but Dad was getting impatient. Downing another beer as we talked at home after a race, he wanted me to go faster, try harder and damn it, "Drive like a man." He was so tough and so confident I just wanted to make him proud. If Dad said jump off an eight-foot ladder I would not even question him; I would jump to show him how tough I was.

Later that winter at Jolly Rogers I began riding the Yamaha 80 my Dad bought for my brother — he wouldn't ride it — and I had a little more power, confidence and ability. I remember well one race in particular from this period where my new confidence paid off.

The green flag dropped and I slammed the gears, sliding back on the seat to get better traction and — largely due to being so much smaller and lighter — I shot into turn 1 as the leader. That was kind of cool, I thought. I'm not getting dusted out, my hands are not getting rocked: I'm out front. Feeling like a rabbit being chased by hounds, I did everything I could to avoid crashing and not get passed. A few laps later I was still out front and feeling a little bold, I got the front wheel off the ground about six inches when I went over start-finish jump. Better yet, Dad was still watching me race and he even seemed interested as I passed by each lap.

After taking the checkered flag in first place — my first win! — I rode back to our truck and parked the bike. Dad greeted me with a big smile and then he hit me with his hand on the back of the head and said "Not bad, meathead." That was his idea of affection; at least the helmet was still on my head or I might have been confused. Several weeks later we went back to Jolly Rogers and I pulled off a second-place finish, another trophy! Another whap to the head!

CHAPTER 5 — MORE LESSONS LEARNED

One day while we were living in Federal Way my Dad announced he had decided to buy a Yamaha 360; his 175 just did not have the power or speed anymore. This new 360 was a monster, silver/gray in color and bad nasty fast. Terry also purchased a new 360 so he and Dad would again have the same bike and riding experience.

I thought at the time that Dad's new bike would mean we would get to go riding more often, but this was not the case. He would go riding with Terry or some of his other buddies and leave me at home. Watching him leave without me was crushing. To make me feel better about staying home, Dad would always say, "You will go on the next ride, for sure." Once in a while he and Terry would take me along, but I rarely met Dad's expectations riding away from a race track so I would end up at home more often than not. During one of those rare riding opportunities I got to go along on, Dad put me up to drag racing Terry, me on my 80 and Terry on his 360. On paper this was not a good match-up, but I think I was able to beat Terry four out of five races. I recall Terry was mildly impressed and puzzled all at the same time.

By this time I was becoming a more capable rider and with my very small body size "at the time" I was often able to win the holeshot — be the first rider to get through the first turn — in races. I learned how to get the most of the machines I was riding. I think Dad saw something in my ability at that time as it became a riding ritual to have him put me up against more experienced riders on bigger bikes. As I continued to improve and Dad started to talk about racing on more tracks and having me compete at a higher level, racing experiences with him started to be fun.

Now with a few races behind me, my priority shifted from just getting to go ride somewhere to seeking out anything that even resembled a track I could practice on. Occasionally, Dad had an odd way of teaching me lessons and one lesson in particular proved to be unforgettable. It happened on another one of those rare trips where I was allowed to go with my father, this time to a riding area with trails and a small, unmaintained track.

When we pulled into this riding area, I immediately noticed a very rocky and bumpy scramble track close to where we parked. By this time I was much more interested in track racing than trail riding and hill climbs. On the other hand, Dad wanted to ride trails and hill climb, partly because by then he could not keep up with me on a track, even when he was on the 360 and I was riding the 80. Not being the hill-climbing go-getter Dad wanted me to be — I was a racer — I decided to hit the track.

This track was rougher than I was used to but I was determined to figure out how to be fast. I spent several hours on the track while the others from our group rode trails and hills, and on one of my faster laps I crashed about forty yards away from where our truck was parked. Dad and some of the others had gathered there to watch me hot lap.

The crash was not terribly bad but I ended up under the motorcycle at an odd angle — my head downhill and the bike on my legs up to my waist — with the exhaust pipe burning me. Still being pretty small I was not strong enough to lift the bike off of me at that odd angle and I cried out several times for help. My Dad watched me intently but did not move. I wanted — needed — to get the bike off me right then, but the burning hurt only half as much as the pain I felt when I realized my Dad was not going to come to my aid.

Someone from our group finally came over to pick up the bike and help me back to the truck. The burn on my leg was not bad but a great deal of skin was peeled off my left arm as a result of contact with the ground; I was bleeding and the wound was packed full of dirt. Dad, who had been drinking a great deal by this point, said "Hey, meathead, get over here," and directed me to stand beside him.

I could tell he was disappointed because I was not acting like the man he expected. I was crying, mostly from the hurt of realizing he would not come to my aid when I needed him, and I didn't want to get back on the bike or stand next to him because I did not trust him. Dad grabbed my arm and poured some beer on my wound. When I tried to pull away he held my arm tightly and poured what was left of his beer onto my arm, telling me with mild disgust in his voice to act like a man. I was 8 or 9.

Moving to Federal Way also gave me another life lesson. When we lived there it was not uncommon for Dad to come home intoxicated where he could generally be meaner than usual, more aggressive and all-around scary to 7-9 year old children. One night he came into the house in a flaming rage, blood all over his face and hands, screaming for Mom who had already left in a big hurry for some reason.

Calming down to console us, he said Mom was going to move away and we now would have so much fun, we would go racing and riding all the time, that is what we would do. When we move to a new house we will get new motorcycles for us three and life would be so much better.

Then the switch flipped again and he was back in a rage, pacing through the house, hiding guns and barking orders at us. He paused for a moment and then the switch flipped again. Dad sat my brother and I down and told us the police would likely be at the house shortly, he might get arrested and if he was, not to be scared because he will have Grandma Dana come get us.

We were still pretty young to understand any of what had happened to bring all of this on and to our home, but I recall we had been locked out of the house a couple times in Federal Way, also. I don't recall if the police came into our house or if Dad went outside to talk to them. Mom came home after a couple of days, but I recall things were pretty tense for a few weeks around the house.

Around the same time, a big part of Dad's training program for riding consisted of antagonizing, taunting and teasing me, as if these would somehow magically prompt me to ride better or try harder. This was always the way it was riding with him away from the track, which made those experiences bittersweet.

Not long before we moved away from Federal Way, on our last trip to the Federal Way Pit site, we were parked near a jumping area with 20 to 30 paths up a hill of varied steepness. The mostly rocky hill was about 30 feet tall and had a flat hard surface. Good riders would launch off the edge of the hill and fly as high as 15 to 20 feet in the air and probably 40 to 60 feet out, landing hard on the flat surface. I had been trying to fly in the air like the talented riders we saw, however I was getting only about 2 to 4 feet in the air and the little Yamaha 80 with its 3 inches of shock travel provided a brutally hard landing.

Dad had been hydrating with Rainier beer, his drink of choice then, and when I came back to the truck to rest after about 20 or 30 jumps that were not to his satisfaction, he blasted me for riding like a sissy and told me I needed to learn to ride like a man. I was crushed and after what seemed like 10 minutes of taunting he said "Put your hat back on and follow me, I will teach you how to jump." Now Dad fancied himself as a very accomplished rider and racer, this without ever winning a single trophy in I don't know how many races he entered. My own view was every time he got on a motorcycle he and his bike usually came home busted and bruised.

At that point all I wanted was to load the bikes and go home, but he made it clear we were not going home until he showed me how to jump and I proved I could do it. Sensing I would maybe get the belt, I decided to launch the bike harder than I ever had before just to get him off this rant.

I was parked some distance from the edge of the jump with instructions to watch him intently as he would teach me how to fly a motorcycle. I heard him launch the bike below the hill, second gear, third gear and then fourth gear — and I sensed I was about to see something amazing because after all he was Superman to me. As the bright red new Husqvarna left the edge of the jump flying upwards it took me a moment to realize he was not connected to the bike but rather flying behind it about five feet or so.

I could see clearly under the bike as it seemed so much higher in the air then it should be, and as it began the slow graceful fall back to the concrete-like flat rocky surface dad was still five feet behind, flying with his feet forward and arms flailing behind his head. As if synchronized, he and the bike hit the ground at nearly the same moment and fenders and pieces of the brand-new bike went flying everywhere.

I was instantly panicked when I saw Dad twisting on the ground in severe pain and others who saw the crash instantly ran to him to inventory his wounds. As I got near him I could tell he was gasping for breath and reaching around to his lower back. A couple folks suggested getting an ambulance and then as if he was Superman, Dad told them he didn't need any help, he was fine. But he had pain etched on his face and I knew it was probably serious. The bike was a mess, too.

Dad lay on the ground for a few minutes to catch his breath, and when he was ready to stand someone grabbed each arm to help get him upright. He groaned with pain just moving and when Dad was nearly straight up he reached around to feel his butt, finding a hole torn in his riding leathers all the way through to his skin. Seeing his bare butt hanging out for all to see gave everyone there a hearty laugh, but I also saw traces of blood seeping through his torn underwear. Numbed by the beer, Dad managed to laugh a little but riding and my lesson were done for the day.

Not that I was anything special as a rider at that time, but I think it did finally occur to Dad he probably wasn't helping to improve my riding with stunts like that. Never again did he attempt to show me how to ride.

CHAPTER 6 — 1974

In 1974 we moved again. Dad came in one day and told the family we were selling the house and moving to Rochester, Washington. As he always did, he told us about how great living in Rochester would be, how much fun we would have. We were buying a brand-new house this time, but before I could open my mouth to ask he told me I wouldn't be getting my own room. Instead, he said a room would be made for me to sleep in the garage, but until that happened I would share a room with my brother.

It took two years before the room in the garage was built for me and I spent those couple years sleeping on a couch or in my brother's room. This stung quite a bit: my little sister got her own room! But what Dad said next made me instantly forget all about not having my own room.

Dad told me the good news was the backyard at the new house was big enough, one acre, for me to build a practice track. I nearly thought I had gone to heaven when I heard those words: my own track in my own backyard. I didn't know how big an acre was, but it sounded so darn big! You can ride anytime you want, Dad said, and you can plan on racing all the time. I wasn't pleased about not having a bedroom of my own, but a track of my own more than made up for it.

The Rochester house was new, a three-bedroom rambler with a bright yellow exterior and a backyard that was a whole acre of weeds and rocks. It was also just one block from the Maple Lane Prison.

We moved into that house in early winter, late October or early November, so the days had turned gray, cold and damp, making my potential track a muddy, rocky mess. The only thought on my mind was to start working on the track, or if nothing else at least just ride in the backyard and pretend I had a track. But Dad would say, "No, too muddy," and that we would build a track later when the weather improved.

The first nice day of early spring, when I could at last ride in the backyard and start making my track, ended abruptly when the neighbor next door came over and complained. Dad then said we would be planting a garden instead.

I continued to improve as a racer and Dad continued to modify my Yamaha 80 in an attempt to make more power and make it look cool. What he was thinking when he painted it baby blue I will never know, but I still remember how embarrassing it was to bring that bike to a track. Over the winter we started making it to more races at Straddle Line and a couple other local tracks, but we were getting our butts kicked because I could not practice enough and Dad's improvements often backfired.

The Honda XR 75 was the bike all the fast kids were racing and winning with and I thought without one I'd never get better as a rider. The XR 75 had a sleek silver tank and fenders, and a low profile seat; replace the stock factory pipe with a Bassini or DG Pipe and you had the coolest-sounding bike ever! After many months of pleading my case with Dad that I would be so much better with an XR 75, he finally agreed to buy me one. I think he realized his efforts to make the Yamaha faster were for naught. We traded the Yamaha 80 and sold the 60 because at this point my brother still did not like riding or racing.

That amazing mellow four-stroke sound, that shiny new silver tank, a slim seat, cool flat fenders — I was beyond obsessed with my new XR 75 and it showed on and off the track. The first few races we participated in with the XR 75, scrambles and flat-track competitions, I finished towards the front of the pack. We added the flat track at Rainier, Washington, to our schedule and it did not take long for me to be running near the front there as well. By this point my Dad and I were off to some track or the other on Wednesday and Friday nights, and all day Saturday, and boy, we started winning.

Still determined to get me more horsepower and performance, Dad and I both were learning expensive lessons. He was learning that trying to make more horsepower was difficult without lots of money and experience, and I was learning how much it sucked to break down all the time, especially when the XR 75 was one of the most reliable bikes competing at that time.

Looking back on it now that period of time was somewhat ideal. Mom and Dad seemed to be getting along great, I don't recall getting locked out of the house anymore, my little sister was still way too small so Mom was tied up with her, and my brother did not care much about racing. It was me and my Dad most of the time and we kicked ass! He wasn't calling me meathead everyday anymore, and he and I seemed to enjoy being together and competing. We were a team and I found real joy in racing with my Dad.

Before long I had 20 trophies on the mantel and when we showed up at a track we were the real deal, we were competitive. Keep in mind we did not have the money many of the other fast riders had, so we did not have a fancy trailer or van, tools, crazy paint job and cool riding gear. It was me and Dad with a little tool kit, a can of gas and about $15 so we could get into the track and maybe have a snack. Dad was never all that good a rider, but he did try his best to be a great crew chief. Sometimes he was, but at other times he had a few too many beers and was not that great a crew chief. It was always exciting to find out which crew chief I was going to have.

Rochester also had a few life lessons to give. By the middle of summer I still had no track of my own in the backyard, but from time to time I would convince Dad to let me ride there so I had worn a trail into the perimeter. Then my brother, sister and I went on a trip to California to see my mother's mom, our grandmother. No problem, I thought. Disneyland, Knott's Berry Farm — pretty cool stuff for a 12 year old knocking on the door of 13.

After 10 days or so we returned home for me to find my cousin Peter, a likeable goof, had built a track in our backyard where he and my Dad practiced together. Not only that, but Peter was sleeping in my couch/ bed. Dad would never let me build the track he promised I could have, he never practiced with me and then, insult of all insults, my cousin said he and Dad also went riding a couple of times at a place in Centralia called Yard Birds. My Dad would never take me there! Ever! I was so jealous, so upset, so hurt and on top of it to my mind Peter was a terrible rider! Heck, he couldn't do anything well when it came to riding.

I was simply crushed, but that wasn't the only bad experience that summer.

In late August there was an escape from the prison that was just one block from our house. At that time my unofficial bedroom was still the couch,

26

and around two in the morning someone came to the glass door a mere 10 feet from where I was sleeping. We couldn't lock that door because Dad ran the antenna wire for our family TV through the doorway and up to the roof along the outside of the house.

As I lay on the couch I heard a person at the door, heard him opening the door, and I was paralyzed with fear. I wanted to scream but my mouth would not open. The door opened, he came in a couple of steps and then stopped. I could only see the silhouette in the dark, but I recall he appeared bigger than Dad. The man turned around suddenly and left, leaving the door partially open, but I could not move for what seemed like five minutes. I was terrified.

Finally I got the courage to get up and run to my parent's bedroom where I told them what happened. Dad said, "You meathead, it was only a dream," and added I was scared of my own shadow. Mom stopped him and said she thought she heard something and that our dog Sally, who was chained up, had been barking a lot in the last half hour or so. With frustration, Dad got up and looked around in the house and then he went into the garage where he grabbed a garden shovel and barked at me to go outside with him. Dad made me walk around the house with him to prove to me no one was there.

We learned later from a neighbor that several men had escaped the prison that night.

CHAPTER 7 — THE BIGGEST RACE OF MY CAREER TO DATE

Dad and I had our ups and downs with racing. If I won, things were usually great regardless of how much beer he drank. Finishing third or worse, I was barely worth talking to, even if I rode my heart out.

On average we were getting better, though. We were now racing in the Expert class and competing each and every time we showed up. This success was bittersweet because the cost was impacting the family in every way, but we were becoming so competitive Dad would spend money he didn't have to make sure we could race, and occasionally we talked about turning pro. If we were going to compete at that level we needed more horsepower, better equipment, and an edge of some kind because we did not have the money or expertise of the guys we would be racing against. Dad was constantly trying to modify my bike, thinking he could find the power we could not afford to buy, but this usually ended up not working out.

This turned out to be the case for the biggest race of my young career to that point.

It was towards the end of the summer in 1975, perhaps Labor Day weekend, and racers from all over the region were set to descend on Straddle Line, Grays Harbor County, for a three-day event. Dad and I talked about this race every night the week leading up to the event. Different types of races were scheduled each day — Flat Track Friday, Scrambles Saturday and Motocross Sunday — with nightly and overall class winners. We figured I would stand a good chance of placing very high overall and towards the top of each event. Both of us thought I had a real shot at winning the flat-track event and being near the top in the scrambles, so for motocross I would just need to be in the top-10.

But two hours before we were set to leave on Friday, Dad got a call: Grandma Dana, his mother, had had a heart attack. Dad said he would have to leave for Seattle, but my Mom and Grandma Dottie would take me to the racetrack. I was not happy about this, but Dad said he would make it for the

28

next day's race. I could tell he was not pleased with the idea of missing the first day, flat track was my best event. Dad was irritable, frustrated and also highly concerned for his mother.

He had also recently been experimenting on my motor, looking for more power, and my bike would not always run well after pumping it up so many times. Dad usually figured it out, but there was always a little uncertainty about what would happen every time we went to the track.

So, there I was. A 12 year old heading out to the biggest race of my life and I realize Mom, Grandma and I together are not strong enough to lift the bike up into the back of the truck. A neighbor was asked to help, but it was not a great start. I admit, when we entered the track I was not feeling as cocky and full of myself with my Mom and grandmother, both two inches shy of five-foot tall, as my pit crew.

The buddies I raced with noticed my father was not with us, and several of their dads offered to help out. Hoping Mom and Grandma would not embarrass me, I kept thinking to myself: *I can do this, I don't need anyone, I don't need any help, I can do this!*

I fired up my bike, getting as a reward the nice, mellow sound of a four-stroke single cylinder engine, and idled over to the pit staging area. Waiting for me there were some of the best riders in the region, guys I had heard of but never seen race before.

In the drivers meeting, we learned heat races would be 19 laps instead of the usual 15 and the finishing order of the heat would set the starting grid for the final. I drew a bad lane for my heat, but knew with a good start I could run to the outside and gain track position.

The flagman dropped the green and off I went, coming out of the first turn with the front tire eight inches off the ground and my bike laying over as if I was falling down. I was perfect on air pressure and making good horsepower, and with that great start I found myself in the lead. I started to pull away from the pack and as the laps wound down the gap from me back to the rest of the riders got larger and larger looking over my left shoulder.

Then it was lap 15 or 16 and my bike started to miss and sputter like I was running out of gas. I got past at the start-finish line but going into the

29

first corner the motor died at exactly the wrong place, sending me hard into a plywood fence.

I got up and tried starting the bike — nothing! With tears running down my face I instantly knew what just slipped away from me, the heat race that I had nearly won was now entirely lost. I was dialed-in and beating all those other great riders; I would have started on the pole for the final. The biggest race I ever saw with the best riders in the region and my bike died with two laps to go.

I tried and tried to start the bike, other dads came over to help, but nothing worked. The motor simply would not fire. I had some help pushing the bike to the pits where my buddy's dad, who had lots of money, offered to let me race their spare bike. I sat on it, started it, ran it through the gears in the pits and brought it back to him and said: "No, thank you." I just did not have the feel of that bike and was too upset to even think straight. I was done, I was not going to race that night, and I was not going to race the next day because I didn't have a bike that would run. With help from one of the dads in the pits we loaded my broken bike into the truck and drove home; me, my mother and Grandmother were completely dejected.

Not staying to the end of the race we got home earlier than expected and Dad arrived later that night. Grandma was fine and already home, so he asked what happened. Mom told him the bike broke down and he then asked me what happened. I told him about how I was out front and leading, pulling away, and the bike just died. My brother woke to share the same exact story.

Dad was so mad his face was red. He went out and unloaded the bike in the dark then kicked it over and it started on the first kick — fired right up! I could not believe it; Dad pegged the throttle and the little motor screamed perfectly, not a miss. I am sure our neighbors did not appreciate how well the bike was running at that time of night.

Dad slammed the bike down on the ground and with rage in his eyes he said: "So okay now tell me the truth! What the F happened?" He believed I was running out front and crashed, he didn't want to believe the bike simply stopped running.

No matter what we said, he did not believe either my mother or I, thinking instead we were both lying to him to cover up a riding mistake. That night just before we went back to bed he said we were not racing anymore and were selling the bike. The next few days were absolute torture for me; first for not being able to compete in this huge event and second knowing he would be selling my bike. I wanted to race so badly and tested his interest by asking if we could at least race the last two events, but Dad antagonized and taunted me, reminding me the bike didn't run right. A few weeks later he sold my bike and I was crushed for weeks.

A piece of me left that day, along with my willingness to trust my father.

CHAPTER 8 — ALASKA?

In the fall of 1975 Dad told us: "Guess what! We are moving to Alaska!" He said it was paradise; we could fish and hunt, ride motorcycles and snow machines — and we could race! After getting there and settling in we would buy new bikes and snow machines and it would be paradise.

Once again I had to learn/deal with saying goodbye to friends and it was the worst feeling. I desperately wanted to stay connected to my friends, especially my classmate Lydia, who I was smitten with, and I did not want to be 2,000 miles away even if we were moving to paradise.

We moved to Anchorage in November, and it was cold, icy and there was no snow on the ground anywhere but the ground was frozen solid. Mom and Dad had found us a house but it was not yet complete; those were boom days and demand for housing was incredible as workers affiliated with the Trans-Alaska Pipeline needed places to live. The local economy was red-hot because most of those workers were making great money and houses were selling for double what they were worth in Washington.

The good news was when the new house was done I would get my own room! The bad news was we would live in an apartment until the house was ready. The apartment complex we moved into was called Dana Apartments — a funny coincidence but there was no relationship. We finally moved into the new house on Alpine Drive, where finally I would get my own bedroom downstairs, just before Christmas 1975. The house was brand new, bigger than any house we had ever lived in, and it was in fact pretty close to paradise when it snowed.

The new year was 1976, America's Bicentennial, and one day that spring Dad came home and told me to take a look in the back of the truck. I did and nearly broke the front door down on my way out to see a shiny new red Honda XR 80 — so cool!

Dad said over the winter there would be an indoor flat-track race in a nearby sports arena; I think it was called Sullivan Arena. He said famous flat-track racer Squeaks O'Conner was promoting the event and also racing in it.

To get ready for racing in a hockey rink on concrete surrounded by plywood walls, Dad, with moral support from me, made some changes to the new red XR 80, adding a new tailpipe and aircleaner, and changing gears. I had never raced on concrete before and even though Dad was convinced he knew how to coach me, as it turned out he was wrong. I would need some time and a few dozen laps to figure the new surface out, so when I started my first race I had little to no expectations. Dad on the other hand was confident I would tear it up.

It came as a complete shock and surprise to me, maybe not Dad, but I won the event, competing on my little XR 80 in the class above me, 125cc Amateur. I raced a couple more times in the 125 Amateur class and won, prompting the promoter to ask Dad if I could run in the 125 Pro class. Dad agreed and allowed me to run out of class, but it took only one race and Dad started to show signs of being uncomfortable with the speed and contact for my size and bike. I won those races, too, but I was also getting treated for concrete burns, bruises and getting hurt nearly every time I got out on the track. The older Pro riders did not enjoy having me in their class.

After two or three of these races Dad decided the move up to the Pro class was too rough for me and I was in danger of getting seriously hurt. This was unusual for my Dad to openly show concern for my health, so it must have been really bad.

So Dad told my brother and I that we were going to make a change. My brother would get the XR 80 and I would get a YZ 80. This came as a bit of a shock to me. A YZ 80? It wasn't a Honda, and I was not sure how it would work out. Dad had the habit of making equipment decisions I knew little or nothing about, but if he said something was good, I wanted to believe it was good. But this was not always the case, and the YZ 80 was an example.

I rode the bike a few times in the mud, slush and snow before conditions around the house made it impossible to ride — Alaskans call that "break up," several weeks of snow melt slush that is just nasty — but try as I might, I did not like the YZ 80. The power band was too soft, it had little torque and it was just not comfortable for me to ride; it was not me! I couldn't make the bike perform and Dad would often comment, "Hey meathead, you look like a monkey humping a football" when I rode it.

Undaunted, after "break up" we went to a track, Kincaid Park, for one of the first races of the season. It was a pleasant warm day for Anchorage in the spring. The track was nothing more than a giant sand pit with a little bit of dirt in a few places. Sand was another surface I had no experience with and on top of that now I was riding a machine I was not comfortable with.

During the first practice I was fast but getting beat soundly by the guys riding Suzuki's new RM 80 and the three or four racers riding XR 80s. Even so, I finished near the front, I think third, in the first moto. By that time Dad had been hydrating with his drink of choice, cold beer. This was not new but still he was unusually antagonistic, taunting me in front of the other racers and their fathers. He asked me why I could not keep pace with the fast guys, and as I was now a smart-ass teenager my response was not at all what he wanted to hear. Frustrated with the situation, I said "I don't know, maybe there's something wrong with the motor."

Instant rage! Dad replied: "Let me see that thing" and he stepped up to the bike, pushing me away from it and nearly knocking me to the ground. He started it and twisted the throttle wide open for two or three minutes with a smirk on his face until the motor simply blew up. Then Dad sarcastically bellowed for everyone who happened to be watching this spectacle to hear: "Son, you're right! There is something wrong with the f-ing motor" as he let the bike fall to the ground and walked to the back of the truck to grab another beer. The sounds of the track and racing seemed to fade away at that moment and those nearby walked away shaking their heads in disgust.

This degree of obnoxious behavior I was pretty accustomed to in private and occasionally in full view of fellow racers or riders, but this was unusually mean-spirited and the images of that day still live with me.

Once again things were pretty tense around the house for a couple weeks after that, not a lot to talk about, not a lot to do, but one day Dad called my brother and I upstairs to the kitchen for a family conversation. We had not raced since that incident at Kincaid Park and I had no idea what he was thinking or planning. He was still angry I was not comfortable on the YZ

80, so out of the blue Dad said we would trade in the XR 80 and YZ 80 for two new Suzuki RM 80s.

Although happy with the idea, I was also concerned. What would happen if I couldn't figure out how to be fast and win with the RM 80? I was already thinking about what stunt he might pull this time to show everyone he was the omnipotent one and his kid was the meathead, as he so affectionately nicknamed me. In the end I was prepared to make the best of it because I wanted to race and getting called names was a small price to pay.

First time on the bike it did not take long for me or Dad to realize the RM 80 fit me like a glove. Not only did I start winning races but I started winning by big margins. With the confidence gained from doing so well, we made the decision to compete for the state championship. Going for the title meant traveling to Soldotna and Fairbanks, over 1,000 miles all total, to race and in 1977 I ended up third overall in the state of Alaska in the 80 class.

I still have that trophy today and I think Dad was proud, but the Soldotna race changed my life forever, and his perspective on racing possibly as well.

In preparation for our trip to Soldotna Dad had been tuning on both of the RM 80s as was a pre-race custom. At this time I was having a recurring problem with the throttle on my bike sticking wide open during races. Dad's solution at the track was to ride the kill button — we won those races, too! — but he vowed to fix it before the big State Championship race.

One evening after work and after several frosty ones, he took a crack at repairing this nagging problem. Proud of his handiwork, he kicked the 80cc two-stroke motor to life and ran up the RPMs a few times to make sure the throttle would not stick. Wanting to avoid blowing this motor up, he decided to take the bike down the dirt road 200 feet or so and then on the return trip peg the little motor wide open to fully test the repair.

At 5-foot-10 and 200-plus pounds, Dad probably thought he could handle anything the RM 80 could muster, but that small machine was deceptively powerful and fast. After making a slow, lazy turn to allow a little more heat to get into the motor before the trip back to the house, Dad twisted the throttle all the way back and the nose of the machine jumped out up like a rocket launching! Wow, my brother and I noted as we watched the tiny bike jump into the air after hitting the tail bar, tearing the rear fender off and bending the handle bars in a cloud of dust, smoke and fading engine noise.

Like the Terminator, Dad lifted himself up off the ground and he began walking towards the house, leaving the bike lying on its side in the middle of the road as he surveyed the blood coming through the elbows of his long-sleeved shirt. We noticed he was walking in a most odd way however, as if he was badly hurt. Then it occurred to us as my brother and I fell down laughing and rolling in the grass: he tore both heels off his cowboy boots when he went over backwards! He was walking rather awkwardly because his cowboy boots had no heels!

As Dad walked by us, still on the ground holding our stomachs, he said softly "Go get the bike, the throttle is fine."

Soldotna, Alaska was a beautiful place to live or just visit. With the emerald blue-green water of the Kenai River, hunting and amazing fishing, it was a paradise for the outdoor enthusiast. When we arrived at the track for the two-day event I was expecting it to be small — small town, small track — but it turned out to be huge, lots of room to race but also a rough surface. Dad and I had heard there were some very fast riders at this track, and we were about to learn that rumor was true. During a brief practice session to get familiar with the track, I was able to keep pace with the fastest three riders in my class. This was encouraging because this was a new track for me, not them, so they had a sizable advantage on me.

In the first of two motos on day one I got the holeshot and was first into turn one off the start, braking hard, tires barely on the ground because it was so rough. I rolled through the first turn on the rear wheel with the lead, feeling slightly confident. At that very moment I caught a rut and the rear tire came up off the ground and then the front tire dug in. It happened so fast that I recall only that my left knee took the entire impact directly.

I knew instantly that I was hurt, but did not know how bad so I stood the bike up and started it. I was going to return to the race and see if I could maybe make a run from the back of the pack and salvage a decent finish.

Something was wrong with my knee, however, and I needed to keep my leg straight, I could not sit down or bend my leg. I finished the race standing up, holding my leg straight. I could feel my knee swelling in my race pants.

After the checkered flag I drove into the pits, where Dad was mad as hell. He called me a quitter and a pussy and taunted me, encouraging me just to quit the race so we could go home. While he was calling me names, Mom calmly asked me to let her see my knee because she could tell it was swollen. I tried to take the racing pants off and could not pull them over my knee, so Mom and Dad working as a team took scissors or a knife and cut them off. Once Dad saw my knee he backed off on calling me names. Over the years this, too, was a customary way of communicating his frustration: moving away from verbal diatribes to silence when he was angry.

Dad fixed my bike for the second moto but my knee was the size of a small watermelon. He did not think the medics needed to look at it, so instead we came up with a race plan. Dad decided I would race in jeans with a hole cut in the knee and taped over; no knee pads or protection. Needless to say I did not run my best race that afternoon as I was afraid to wreck without protection while my knee was injured. By this time I was not having much fun, but I somehow managed a third-place finish for Saturday, day one.

When Sunday morning arrived, my knee was bruised badly and still swollen, and Dad realized I should not race without protective gear on my legs. My brother was also racing, so he let me wear his racing pants with knee pads — my hand-me-downs — giving me some protective gear and a little confidence. Pumped up with aspirin and ice on the knee, I was feeling pretty good and with some luck we figured I could possibly get a top-five finish.

The brief practice session we had on Sunday did little to loosen my knee up but I still had the desire to race so I lined up for the first of two motos. At the drop of the green flag I was off, making it into turn one first but I slowed down and lost a couple spots the moment I needed to use my knee to get through the turn. Despite gaining a little confidence from my brother's race pants, mentally I did not have the strength or will to push the injury too hard; I was frankly scared. I ran the rest of the moto going back and forth between third and fifth place, getting more and more frustrated that I could not catch the front runners or when I was passed on a long straight by a rider who would normally be slower than me.

I finished the first moto in third or fourth and returned to the pits to talk to Dad. All things considered, I felt pretty good about the finish but Dad blasted me. He was angry I was not riding harder.

The second moto of the day was the last race of the event for our class. Sitting at the starting gate with about 30 seconds to go before the green flag, something clicked and I decided I would try to win that damn race! I somehow rationalized my knee would not be able to take the pounding on the jumps but I could fight through it and make up time on the straights with very rough bumps called whoops.

The green flag dropped and I headed into the first turn in the middle of the pack. I climbed into the top five after a few laps and feeling a bit more confident, I began to push a little harder. On the long straight in the back of the track I pushed harder and harder, jumping from one whoop to another wide open in fifth gear when my knee gave out.

I plowed into the next whoop and that drove me off the track to the right. I landed in a six-foot depression, face first with the bike hitting me in the back, and as the bike pitched forward over my head my legs became caught in the handle bars, flipping me like a rag doll. I had no air in my lungs and my face was packed full of Soldotna sand; I was hurt, nothing broken, but I was hurt and not able to catch my breath.

Track helpers began waving flags instantly and Dad ran from the pits to the site of the wreck, about 300 yards, in what seemed like 10 seconds. When he got to me, Dad could see the wreck was bad and he barked at the safety guys to help me. It was the first time in the 150 or so races that Dad and I had gone to together that he was shaken by a violent crash. I had many crashes, but years later he told me that was the first one that shook him up.

Knowing how upset Dad would be if I did not finish this race, I asked him to start the bike for me while I was trying to catch my breath and taking inventory of my bruises and bleeding. For the first time Dad said I did not need to finish the race, but I asked him again if the bike would run. He started it and with bent handle bars and broken levers I finished the race in first or second gear, just idling around the track until the Moto was completed.

The trip home was very subdued. We did not talk a great deal but both of us knew I just lost my chance at the 1977 state championship. Although we never spoke about it, I think he and I also knew my mental edge was also lost; I was afraid, very afraid, of getting hurt again.

CHAPTER 9 — WHERE THE HECK IS NENANA?

Sure enough, four months later it happened yet again: "Guess what? We are going to move again," Dad told us in March 1978. He was excited about it, saying we were moving to a great little Alaskan village called Nenana to live in a one-room log cabin and maybe we could get new motorcycles again. Sure enough, he decided to sell our bikes again.

Don't get me wrong, Nenana was a wonderful little town and I met my first love there. But I also experienced amazing things like the smell of rotting fish, piles of fish guts and rusty tap water that smelled like sulphur. It was as if our water supply contained a hundred junk cars and a million boiled eggs and you got to enjoy that aroma every time you showered or brushed your teeth.

Significantly, another of my new experiences in Nenana was learning to consume large quantities of beer as my Dad had educated me on the fine art of hydrating with a tasty libation. Late winter and early spring there just was not all that much for a 13-year-old boy to do in Nenana; however I did learn I was able to drink 10 to 12 beers before throwing up. One morning Dad walked around the corner in our cabin to find me passed out in front of the heater with puke all around me. It was how the youth passed the time in Nenana back in the day; I am sure that has changed by now.

We had lived in our one-bedroom log cabin only a month or so before I realized Dad and I were growing apart. The void may have been racing, it may have just been life with me getting older and seeing the world differently. In my eyes, life was still all about motorcycles and to my Dad's credit he realized quickly Nenana was not an environment I would do well in without something to focus on besides developing a tolerance for beer. With a total population of about 500, there was little if anything to do but get into trouble. The solution Dad came up with was to buy us new motorcycles.

He bought me an RM 125 and my brother a YZ 100. They were awesome bikes, great fun. I once again had a purpose: to be fearless with that RM 125. With this new bike I became remarkably confident, constantly searching for jumps or hills where I could ride. The burning desire to compete was still with me.

Mom and Dad could tell I desperately missed my friends in Anchorage, so they arranged a trip for me to see my friend Doug that summer. He and I rode our motorcycles all over the hills above town and even took them into Anchorage to ride. We found a jump at Service-Hanshew High School where we were able to get 20 feet into the air and do wheelies from first to sixth gear. It was freedom and joy for us to ride all day long like that; one of the rare moments I got to ride and just have fun, no trophies, just two buddies without a care or fear.

Back in Nenana, I was out goofing around one day when Dad noticed I was getting pretty good with the RM 125. He could sense I wanted to race again and I think he did, too. One day late in the summer he asked me if I wanted to go to Fairbanks to race at the fairgrounds if he could manage to get a break from work. He worked all day every day during summer so this would be a rare moment for him to get the time off. I said "absolutely" and we loaded the RM 125 in the truck and drove the 55 miles to Fairbanks.

Neither of us knew what we were getting ourselves into, however. We had the idea that I would race on the big flat-track course there, but not much more than that. Anyone who knows anything about motorcycle racing can tell you not to flat-track race a two-stroke; you'll just embarrass yourself. But Dad had done this to me too many times to count; his lack of race knowledge always hurt us. Too many times he would put me in the wrong venue with the wrong equipment and then get mad because I did not perform.

When we got to the track the race officials took one look at my bike and said I had the wrong pegs and tires, and I could not have a front brake. Dad asked them if we could buy a new rear tire inside the event and would we pass technical inspection by taping the pegs and pulling the brake lever. The official said we could probably do all that, but we definitely needed new tires, no fender and a few other things.

Dad let the truck roll forward about 40 feet and then pulled over to the side of the gravel road so others could drive around us. We looked at each other, he looked in his wallet to count his money to see if he had enough for us to buy the tires and things got very quiet for a minute or two. I knew Dad was going to have to spend another $200-300 that he didn't have to get us race ready and even then I would be competing on a two-stroke against a field of big four-stroke thumper motors. He looked at me and said "If you really want to do this, it's okay."

We had from time to time won many tough races; he believed in me enough to make the commitment of time and money and I believed enough in him that he would get the bike ready in time for the first race. I was, however, concerned what price I would have to pay if I was not competitive. I was old enough then to know I didn't want it to be a train wreck like so many other times in the past trying to race where and when we shouldn't. I turned away from him and looked out the side window, resting my forehead on the glass and said "I don't really want to race, Dad."

Never again did my Dad and I go to a track together to race or even just to watch a race.

That day in Fairbanks was one of saddest and most significant life lessons I could have gotten. I will never forget the sacrifice my Dad made for me to race, how hard he tried to make up for what he did not know and the money we did not have to spend. He would often make magic happen at the track, but in reality it was just his lucky guess or simply just my night. In any event, my Dad and I won nearly 100 races before I retired at the ripe old age of 13. We never won a big race or an underdog victory over someone we shouldn't have been able to beat, but when we raced it was me and my Dad and we won a lot of races and we did have some fun along the way. It was just me and Dad and we had some really great times and we had some really bad times. I love my father dearly and admire him because he truly loved his family and was proud of his family, but at the end of the day he was merely a kid himself raising kids.

Once I turned 16, got a driver's license and the freedom as well as the responsibility that comes with it, I began to develop interests in other things like drums, friends and my wife, who I met in high school and have been married to for 21 years. Like anyone, I often wonder "what if" and look back at those years after that race in Fairbanks. Occasionally, Dad and I talked about doing something else together, usually hunting and fishing. Once in a while we talked about building a hot rod or boat, maybe trying to get into motocross again, but at the end he and I just grew apart. I suppose this is usually what happens between children and their parents.

But I still remember looking out the window of that green 1976 Chevy pickup truck and telling my Dad as I was looking away that I didn't want to race. The truth is I *did* want to race that day. In fact, I still want to race, even today.

CHAPTER 10 — PAM WHO?

Having experienced Nenana, Alaska, during the spring and summer I think Dad noticed my tolerance for beer was pretty high for a 15 year old. He also realized at some point having our five-member family living in a two-room log cabin in a tiny town in remote Alaska would not be a good option for the winter months. So, after he flew to Washington to buy a house, we packed up again and moved to Tenino.

Tenino was 10 miles from Rochester, where we had some friends and it would have been easier for me to reconnect, but for some reason Dad was compelled to move to the other side of the freeway. Dad in his usual fatherly caring way warned me that Tenino was different: the kids were from logging families and were therefore tougher than the pussies in Rochester. If I didn't watch it I would end up with my ass kicked every day.

Armed with this great counsel and many other confidence-building talks from Dad, I decided it would be wise for everyone at Tenino High School to learn real fast I was not to be messed with. It did not take long for me to demonstrate it to my Dad and the school principal, either.

As a freshman I had no tolerance for freshman initiation rituals, so when the senior basketball team wandered the halls looking for first-year students to haze I decided to express my distaste for such vulgar behavior as a freshman in the sights of several marauding seniors.

When one of these seniors, who happened to be the school's superstar basketball player, put oil in my hair over my clear objection, I hit him square in the face. This resulted in me getting stuffed into my locker and hit repeatedly by him and a few others from the team until the varsity basketball coach pulled the superstar basketball player off of me.

The coach promptly grabbed me by the collar, pulled me out of my locker and in a fit of anger dragged me to the principal's office. Both the coach and the principal laid into me for hitting the school's superstar basketball player. As they were telling me all about how much trouble I caused and how I would need to get my attitude under control, I got up and walked out of the school and never looked back.

I made it about four miles when I saw my Dad drive by, headed to the school. He slowed after noticing me walking and quickly spun around in the road and pulled over for me. I got in the car with oil still in my hair.

At this time I was a little old for the belt, so now I was expecting the fist. Instead, we talked on the way home, me telling him what happened. He said he would call the school to get the story on that end. After hearing his side of the discussion during that call, it was pretty clear Tenino High School was no longer an option. Thankfully, Mom and Dad took turns driving me to Rochester for the balance of my freshman year before March when we once again headed back for Dad's job in Nenana to ramp up for the next tug boating season on the Yukon River.

I spent another summer in Nenana, drinking anytime and anywhere to pass the time. I did manage to meet my first love that summer and when she left town for college I was heartbroken. Thankfully and not a moment too soon the summer came to an end. I went to Nenana High School for the first month or so of the school year but once the first snow fell our family moved back to the house in Tenino.

We still had to deal with the school issue, so for the benefit of my parents I decided to give Tenino High another go. It turned out the school had a new principal and the superstar basketball-playing senior had graduated, so things were very different for me this time around. I was glad of this because I wanted to belong to this school — heck, any school at that point. I wanted to be part of the traditions, part of the culture and part of the story; as a part-time student I was none of the above. This was so very frustrating to me for many reasons. I could not comfortably participate in sports or make lasting friendships because I was always moving.

But this time there was something different. I made sure everyone knew I was not to be messed with and much to my shock the most amazing principal, Mr. Maguire, completely supported me when I drilled square in the face one of the jerks in school.

And when I got on the school bus the first day, there she was, this blonde, blue-eyed beauty named Pam. Oh my, did I think she was hot. When I got off the school bus at the end of that day, I met another person who would have a profound impact on my life named Wendell who, as luck would have it, gave me a ride home from the school bus — we had a very long driveway!

It took only a few short weeks of riding the bus with Pam, sitting next to each other going to and from school, for us to realize we liked each other. Not much more time passed and she decided she needed a boyfriend and I needed a girlfriend. Her parents nearly had heart attacks, but if that was not bad enough for them, Pam's sister and my brother also became smitten — but that is truly another book altogether.

I am sure it was only a couple of weeks of being boyfriend and girlfriend before we were no longer a couple. She decided it was not fun being tied down to one boy and promptly dismissed me. I was crushed for weeks and over the balance of my junior and senior years at Tenino we might have spoken 10 words to each other. It was not that we didn't like each other, just that we had nothing in common.

The funny thing is today we still have nothing in common, except our daughter.

As a senior with enough credits to graduate in March of 1981, I made another life choice and it set in motion my life story and the reason I wrote this book. I got a job working for Yutana Barge Lines based in Nenana, for the same owner who usually had heartburn giving my Dad a day off to spend with his family.

The owner was a pompous, arrogant, narcissistic idiot who ended up as the owner because he married the only child of the founder. Had that union not taken hold, I think he would be selling cars at a local car lot, not running a multi-million dollar tug and barge company. Nonetheless, my distaste for the owner was tempered when he let me work on the tugs as a deck hand. I eventually moved up to pilot and sailed as captain on several occasions. Those adventures are also another book entirely, but as I said, this book is not about me, it is about me and my little girl.

It's worth noting that I have a Tenino High School diploma but I received it in a ceremony in Nenana while wearing a wrinkled robe with Tenino's colors and funky disco platform shoes making me at least 5-foot-9. After the ceremony I went out with some friends and drank beer until five the next morning and a few days later I was headed down the Yukon River for the Bering Sea as a deckhand on the MV *Pat*.

The MV *Pat* crew consisted of an Eskimo captain, a really cool pilot, a gay first mate, a punk rocker deckhand and a salty engineer who I connected with and who said he would watch out for me as I was fresh meat! Eventually I ended up on the MV *Tanana* and enjoyed a more normal working relationship and crew. The *Tanana* had an amazing captain and fun crew, and while on board I was much less concerned about losing my other virginity in the wilds of Alaska.

The lifestyle of a single man was great but after several years of seasonal work with Yutana Barge Lines and living in two states, Alaska and Washington, I noticed a trend I was not terribly proud of. I would usually find a girlfriend over the winter in Washington, then in the spring travel back to Alaska. Upon returning to Washington I would usually find the girl I left, who I thought of as my "girlfriend," was dating one of my friends. This was particularly hurtful and difficult with one girl I met and dated from Fairbanks and one girl just out of high school from Oakville, Washington.

To solve this problem, I decided to build a house in Olympia, Washington, as a first step to transitioning from being a gypsy to putting down roots. I enjoyed being single and had many amazing experiences, but by this time I was ready to settle down. My work still required constant travel, so my plan was to find a great companion who would stay in the Olympia house and not be drawn to spend time with my few remaining male friends. Perhaps not the best idea, but it was what I went with.

The house was completed in 1987, a modest little rambler in the woods, private and just right for me and that special person. Who that special person was is something I still did not know at that point, but I was ready to settle down. By 1988, I had the house in Olympia but the rest of my plan was being held up by my job. I was away from my new home most of that summer and in general spending more time somewhere else made it hard to meet someone special.

CHAPTER 11 — A MYSTERY LETTER ON THE YUKON RIVER

In the summer of 1988 I was living and working in Alaska on a dreadful little tug boat named the MV *Yamhill*. The owner at that time had a tendency to embellish when it came to horsepower and size, so although the tug was officially listed as being 90-foot long with 900 horsepower, the reality was much different. About 50 feet and with maybe 500 horses, *Yamhill* was a real pit: no one running the boat before me took care of it or cleaned it. It was a steel-hulled shallow draft vessel and the three-man crew slept together in the bow in bunks that overlapped and gave no privacy.

The generator and main engines were only 20 feet from the living area, which meant the sound level in your bunk was over 100 decibels when the boat was underway. It carried just enough fresh water to give each crew member a shower once a week and it stored enough groceries to last a three-man crew about seven days. This was not a "jewel of the fleet," but I admit it was kind of fun to operate and I did a lot to make *Yamhill* one of the cleanest tugs in the Alaskan fleet.

Steaming to Circle, Alaska, in July at about four miles per hour, the ambient temperature was around the 90-degree mark, so the inside of that cramped, smelly tug would have been over 100. Add to that dense smoke and thick air from the countless forest fires that raged in the region and you get a feeling for what an unpleasant environment sailing in *Yamhill* could be at times.

I recall a few times pulling the tug over to idle along the bank until visibility improved. The fire threat was so strong the company pilot would fly the river ahead of and behind us to report how close the fires were to the river. We had about 10,000 gallons of diesel and 3,000 of gasoline onboard, as I recall.

On this particular trip I had a greater desire to get to Circle than just getting out of the smoke, away from the fires and off the tug for a few hours. I was eager to get to Circle because we were told by the company that the trucks refueling the tug would also deliver mail and some fresh food while we loaded and unload freight.

The truck for the first fuel load was already there waiting when we arrived. After the tug was tied up and the main engines shut down, I walked up to greet the driver, who handed me the mail. We discussed the next fuel deliveries and timing concerns about the fires, and after this brief exchange I headed up to find a phone to call the office. I needed to report our arrival and estimated time for departure, but I also had a personnel matter to discuss with the port captain.

Dusty was not very good at piloting the boat and he was not very good at reading water depths, either, but going downstream he insisted on being in the tug's wheel house and not the pilot boat as I wanted. Dusty claimed he was much better at the helm than piloting, and I was much better in the sounding boat, but I knew if he was driving the tug and barge, now fully loaded with gas and diesel, it was all but certain my tug and crew would land on a gravel bar. To me the decision was based on common sense. Dusty, while young, cocky and likeable enough, didn't have a great deal of talent when it came to running tug boats; instead, he was an artist at building violins. I told the operations manager the situation and he told me to have Dusty call him so it would be made clear to the crewman that Troy would run the tug and he would run the pilot boat.

Walking back to the tug down a dusty road to the riverbank, I noticed that the stack of mail in my hand included a letter addressed to me in handwriting I did not recognize. I opened it up and there was a very well-written letter, in nearly perfect penmanship — and, boy, did it smell good — from someone named Pam. The letter writer went on about how she and her sister stopped by the land next to my house in Olympia and met a guy named Joe who was living there, and how she was hopeful we might reconnect. She also included a couple Tenino phone numbers.

My mind raced. Pam? Pam? I started thinking about how many Pams I knew and would I even want to reconnect with any of them? I raced back to the phone and called Joe, a friend who was watching the house for me, but there was no answer — shit! I called both the numbers in the letter but no one picked up and there was no answering machine — shit! I got back to the tug and found there was still two hours of discharge to go, after which we'd be underway headed back downstream with no phone access for over a week — double shit!

I could not stand not knowing who this Pam was. I needed some sort of information so I made a couple trips back to the phone before departure, but still got no answer from any of the numbers, including my own house in Olympia. Just before we cast off lines I ran back up and tried one last time, but still no answer. I returned to the tug and got ready to head back down river, my curiosity killing me as it would for the next seven days.

After telling Dusty and the deckhand to cut us loose, I eased the now fully-loaded barge off the river bank and began a long slow turnaround so we could point the tow downstream. Once underway I could feel we were a little heavy in the bow and the tow was a little slow to turn. I knew a pilot boat was needed in front of me to locate the channel; this was my first trip on this stretch of river and we had no maps.

About 15 miles downstream from Circle the air became clearer and the muddy brown water of the Yukon began to reflect the setting arctic sun. Dusty was in front of the tug in the 14-foot pilot boat, looking for a channel to keep us in deep water and not aground, and I was at the tug's helm. As we approached a difficult crossing, I watched Dusty run lines out and began to have some concerns that he was putting the tow in the wrong spot by not reading the water correctly. Seeing boils of swirling water ahead and becoming more apprehensive, I pulled the throttles back to idle. I called Dusty on the radio and asked which direction he wanted me to go to avoid the boils, which my experience told me were bad news. He replied that I should leave the boils to my port side and I was nearly yelling when I asked "Port side? You are sure?" He frantically said "Yes, go to starboard! Turn to Starboard! Starboard!"

Even at idle the tug was still making five miles per hour ground speed, meaning I was quickly running out of options and time. Thoughts of going aground and someone naming this tug and barge "Troy Island" ran through my head for a half-second and I told Dusty there was no way I could make it;

50

again, was he sure? He replied with rage in his voice "Yes! Leave them on your port! Port! Port! Go to starboard."

I laid the rudder over hard to starboard, pulled the starboard throttle back and then into reverse then put the port motor full ahead and said "Okay, Dusty, watch my port side," and added that I didn't think we could make it. I was so mad at Dusty that I could have killed him because he waited way too long for me to have time to take a higher line. At that point there was no way to stop; I was committed, thanks to Dusty, but the situation did not look or feel right to me.

As the tug started its slow, lazy turn to starboard Dusty got on the radio and in a barely audible voice, almost a whisper, said: "Sorry boss, I meant port." Instantly I zeroed the rudders, pulled back the port motor to full reverse and then got on the radio. In a rather excited voice I asked Dusty how much water I would have under the tug downstream. He said "Two feet," again in a barely audible voice.

The tug drew four feet so I yelled at the deckhand to hang on, we were going to hit. Just before we made hard contact I got back on the radio to tell Dusty to find me deep water — fast. My plan was to bounce the tug and barge off the gravel bar and to do that I needed to know if there was a hole to drop the tow into.

Dusty slammed the sounding boat into gear and started marking deep water just off the port side. Meanwhile the tug was shaking violently as the propellers began digging into the muddy gravel bar. The deckhand and I could hear gravel slamming into the hull and the bottom of the barge scraping on the bar, then the tug came to an abrupt stop. The barge was hard aground on the starboard side so I put the tug into full reverse and put the rudder over hard to port. The barge just hung there and thoughts of being stuck for days began to creep into my head. At that point Dusty got on the radio to tell me if I get the stern of the tug down under the gravel bar it would just float off. I replied "I'm trying" with contempt in my voice as I had already come to the same conclusion as he bobbed around 50 feet out my window.

With both Cummins motors at full throttle, rocks were pelting the hull of both tug and barge; the vibration was so bad dishes began to fall in the galley and it was so loud we could barely hear ourselves on the radios. All of a sudden the stern dropped downstream, just a few feet at first but then a little more until it started to swing into deeper water — Come on, baby, come on! Half a minute later we were in deep water, pointing the wrong direction in the wrong channel as I tried to avoid losing control of the tow and landing on another gravel bar.

In the midst of this Dusty got on the radio to say "Hey, boss, I think I will just stay in the pilot boat until we get to Fort Yukon if I have to." That made me smile — Fort Yukon was 50 miles away and it was nearly midnight — but to teach him a lesson I left him out there for 25 or 26 miles after we got turned around and headed to Fort Yukon and much better river conditions.

We resumed our trip down the Yukon and then back up the Tanana River to Nenana, where I could get on the phone to find out who Pam was.

Chapter 12 — finding out who pam was: 'the one'

Working six hours on, six hours off, we made good time finishing our run down the Yukon and then up the Tanana River to Nenana, where there would be a phone so I could call to find out who Pam was. I re-read her letter a hundred times over the seven-day trip, trying to recall every girl I knew with the letter P in her name; I was dying to know who she was.

I considered the Pam I met in Coos Bay, Oregon; no, she was mad at me and would not have moved to Washington. I considered one of several Pams I knew from school; no, none of them made sense. Then there was the Pam I met in Idaho once, it could be her; we had a great time but why would she have given me Tenino phone numbers?

Driving a tug for 12 hours a day gives a person a lot of time to think, so right after *Yamhill* settled alongside the dock in Nenana I headed for a phone as fast as a sprinter. I called Joe at my house and bingo! He was home. I asked him about this Pam girl who had stopped by, and he said "Yes, she asked about you, said she knew you so I gave her your address up there so she could write you." I told him that was way too cool, but what was her last name? Joe paused and said "I don't think she said; I don't know!" I asked him what she looked like and he told me she was hot: blonde, blue eyes, smoking hot figure — I must know her if she wrote to me, right? I told Joe I wasn't sure, but I did have a couple phone numbers to try.

I tried the first number from the letter but again, no answer. Calling the second number, I was rewarded at last with a voice on the other end! It was her grandmother, and after telling her who I was I had to ask the ultimate embarrassing question: what's your last name? At long last I found out the mystery girl was Pam Hitzke! But holy cow, that couldn't be true, surely she would be married by now, and surely she would have better things to do than reach out to me?

Pam's grandmother told me she was in California with her parents, but she would let Pam know I called when she returned to Washington. Was there a number for Pam to call me? I only had the tug office number for Pam to call, so I asked her grandmother when she would be back from California. Grandmother wasn't certain, but said it may be the next night. I was so excited and eager to talk to Pam before departing for my next trip — which was up in the air — that I called the next morning and afternoon, finding out both times that she was not yet home.

I finally got the chance to talk to her late the evening before I was scheduled to leave Nenana for another run. We caught each other up on what had happened since we last saw each other, about how and why we were in that place in time. I told her I was an omnipotent tug boat captain and she told me she was a typical California blonde beauty with 1980s big hair.

For reasons I don't recall, we did not get a chance to talk as long as I would have liked and I could not say what exactly we discussed beyond ourselves and our immediate concerns. But I knew she was single, just back from Los Angeles and not sure what she was going to do. I also knew I badly wanted to see her.

We agreed to write each other because I had such limited access to a phone most of the time. I don't recall for sure but our next call was probably a week or two later, with a few letters exchanged. As my bad luck would have it I was being deployed to help a tug make deliveries out in the Bering Sea and Arctic Ocean. This was not a positive from my perspective, but I had some sense of comfort because I could tell we were bonding even though we were 2,000 miles apart. I tried to convince her to fly to Alaska so she could see what I did and maybe take a trip with me, but she was not ready for that.

She was, however, ready to write often and take my calls at any hour while I was in Alaska and the opportunity to find a phone presented itself. She did not know it at the time, but I thought she could be "the one" and if so I was ready to spend the rest of my life with her. I only hoped she felt the same way. Twenty-three years later she is still my soul mate and I am still ready to spend the rest of my life with her.

After about 50 letters, 50 phone calls and 49 attempts to get her to fly to Alaska, that short summer ended in early October and I was just a few days away from seeing Pam, who was going to pick me up at the airport. She had cleaned my house and even stayed there for a few days prior to my return after Joe left. I was so happy and excited that I could barely contain myself during the three-and-a-half hour flight from Fairbanks. I got off the plane and, holy cow, was she hot, I mean smoking hot!

I felt like the luckiest guy in the States, but I was also concerned that my long stay in Alaska without the benefit of female company would possibly cause me to make the wrong impression. I had to constantly remind myself not to be too pushy, not to try to make any moves and for goodness sakes don't act like a stupid fisherman. I failed on all three fronts, but to this day she is still putting up with me, so maybe I really was the luckiest guy in the States at that time.

Maybe, just maybe, I still am.

The covenant of marriage was a concept I thought I understood at that time, and I assured Pam that I could live with. Pam, on the other hand, expressed some measure of trepidation about my ability to truly understand and subscribe to the covenant of marriage, partly because of my gypsy lifestyle and upbringing. Deep down inside I knew the day after we reconnected by phone, me in Nenana and her in Tenino, that she could be the one. I knew the minute I got off the plane, however, that she *was* the one.

We decided to make it official and in October 1990 were married in Lacey, Washington. Pam and I were going to make our lives together the best we could and pursue our dreams. As newlyweds we had our ups and we had our downs, but one thing was sure: she had the confidence and support of her amazing family and I had nothing remotely close to that kind of family support.

If we got into an argument, it was me against five, sometimes more, no questions asked. At first I had some resentment about this but later I learned just how lucky she was and then conversely how lucky I was. Her family was so open, affectionate and loving, while I tried to avoid my family at all costs.

The first time her father tried to give me a hug, I nearly punched him! I was so out of place and felt so alien in that environment that my insecurity put strains on our marriage every day. I was not smart enough to realize that, but fortunately Pam and her family were loving and patient with me and that made me a better husband and, later, father.

CHAPTER 13 — A BABY CARRIAGE FOR A BIRTHDAY PRESENT

Pam and I had the typical newlywed ups and downs — Who does the dishes? Who cleans the house? — and financial challenges. My burgeoning real estate career got off to a very slow start and it did not take long for me to realize I was patently inept when it came to showing and selling houses. I came home one night from an open house and told Pam I thought we were sunk if I had to sell houses for a living. In her very kind and supportive way she said, "I don't care what you have to do, you figure it out."

If I was ever lacking for inspiration all I needed was about 10 minutes with Pam and I was ready to go back out and slay any dragon; partly from my sense of honor as the man of the house and partly to keep my marriage intact. Ten years later I was the CEO of the largest commercial real estate firm in Olympia, Washington, and was one of the region's best known agents for large raw land transactions. I owe this all to Pam's ability to keep me motivated and her constant reminders of our shared priorities.

Our lifestyle for the first few years of marriage made it difficult to think about having a child, so we didn't really see it as an option as we struggled to get our feet under us. But a few years later we started to see things differently when our nephew became part of our lives.

My brother's 3-year-old boy was named Ferris, and he was an adorable boy any father would have been proud to call his son: blonde, blue eyed, full of curiosity, playful and eager to learn. My brother and his then wife were gracious enough to allow Pam and I to have Ferris stay with us on the weekends from time to time. Because my nephew enjoyed spending time with Pam and I so much, at times my brother would ask us to take Ferris because he would occasionally act up if not allowed to see his Aunt Pam and Uncle Troy. We were so blessed to get time with Ferris during the summer and fall of 1993 that we spoiled him every chance we got.

At the same time, I was hinting to Pam that we needed to be thinking about having a kid of our own. Pam, who is the cautious one, methodical and organized to a fault, made excuse after excuse not to have a baby. Finally, getting desperate to win her over on the subject, I came up with a plan. I needed a higher power than me; I needed divine intervention or at least some serious pressure.

I threw Pam a birthday party at our little home in West Olympia and as was the case for every family function, birthday or holiday, her parents along with family and friends came to celebrate with us. As Pam was opening presents, I slipped into the pile a baby stroller I had wrapped and hidden in the spare bedroom. When Pam unwrapped the stroller she looked at me as if I was an idiot — by the way, this was a look I have become pretty familiar with over the years, so it was nothing really new — but her mother reacted perfectly. Mary Ann jumped up and shouted "We're going to have a grandbaby?" She asked Pam if there was a secret to share and then started talking about how wonderful it would be to have another "grandbaby" and everyone at the party began to kid Pam about having a baby.

After the party when we were alone, Pam gently reminded me of our prior agreement not to have a child until we had our finances in order and had some economic stability. I was working hard to make as much money as I could with my real estate career and anything else I could find to make a dollar while Pam was following in her father's footsteps with a career in the Washington State Department of Transportation. Late in 1993 we closed one of the biggest land deals in the area and for the first time that Pam and I had been together we enjoyed some degree of economic security. We went to bed at night not wondering how we were going to pay the bills next month, and felt some optimism that we might make it after all, both in marriage and in the business community.

By January 1994 we were talking frequently (mostly me doing the talking) about trying to have a baby and where our growing family would live. We discussed how we saw ourselves as parents, and how we would handle parenting matters and decisions. Pam, rightfully so, was very concerned about me being too much like my father. The more she considered my childhood, the more reserved she became about getting pregnant. I think Pam could tell based on my interactions with my nephew Ferris and how he

58

responded to me that I was probably going to be an okay dad, and she could tell how much having a child of my own meant to me. Neither of us wanted to place a burden or unrealistic expectations on the other, so as with many open issues we just decided to take it one day at a time.

After so many nights of thoughtful and occasionally vibrant discussion about the future, we decided to build a new house on a property purchased a few years before, and in February we obtained a building permit. That same month, Pam agreed we could start trying for a baby in late March.

Of course I was truly looking forward to doing my part, but somehow — and with military-like precision — Pam turned it into a job with conditions, goals and deadlines. She looked at the days and weeks ahead, planning on the days we would try to make a baby, even going so far as to list a time of day. Over dinner one night Pam pulled out the calendar and marked down the days for optimum conception, telling me it took her sister Kim years to get pregnant and we should not get disappointed if it took too long. By this time I was feeling a little insignificant, but when she yelled "batter up" I was going to be prepared one way or another.

Several weeks passed by and she reminded me: "No, not time yet." A couple more weeks: "No, not time yet." Finally in late March or early April I saw the first date coming up on the calendar and I was eager to get the project started. At the time I was working 16 hours a day, seven days a week building our house, a project so consuming that truthfully neither of us was as focused on making a baby as we had been before starting construction.

One day while I was working at the new house, I think we were framing in the roof, Pam called my cell phone — I had a "brick phone" back then — and she said "Get home now! It's time. You have 30 minutes to get here." I left the new home under construction in a big hurry! As I was headed to our little rental house I pondered how long would this take and would we have a boy or a girl? It was an exciting time.

When I walked in the door I felt like I was being seduced: dinner was cooked and on the table and, oh my, did she look amazing. She was all dressed up and when it was time she was even more dressed up. We did what two loving people do, each performing our respective parts to contribute to the process of making a baby, and later that night we talked about what was going on with our days and workloads. We each agreed we would try for a few months and if nothing happened we would reconsider or hold off for until the new house was complete.

The demands of the house under construction made it impossible for us to reconnect on the next couple of dates marked on Pam's calendar. Both of us were focused on the new house and were not terribly concerned: we figured Mother Nature would do her work in good time. Discussing the timing of when the baby might be born, we decided not to make the effort to connect again the following month when the days were marked. Pam and I agreed we did not want to have a Christmas Baby.

One morning just a mere two or three weeks later while I was still in bed, Pam woke me up, looked at me and said "You are not going to believe this: We are having a baby!" I was laying there in bed and I'm not sure if I even had an expression. Then it occurred to me, damn it, I only got to try to make a baby one time: one shot, one dinner and you get the point. I got over it quickly and Pam made sure family and friends knew we were expecting that day by calling her Mom and Dad first thing.

Pam said she should be born somewhere around Christmas! We both laughed and agreed, as we would always say to each other, that as long as the baby was healthy it wouldn't matter.

The next few months went by quickly. Pam and I were so busy with the new house, my new business was looking promising and, oh yes, we had a baby in the oven. Every night in bed we would discuss things; would we like to know if it's a boy or girl, what names we liked — all the things most first-time parents talk about. Wanting to be surprised, even though we each believed it was a boy, we did finally agree not to have the sex determined with an ultra-sound. Actually, Pam made it a point early on and then stayed the course with how strongly she felt "we" did not want to know before the baby was born if it was a boy or a girl (even though I was a little curious).

We argued playfully every few days about names. Pam wanted Jess or Jessica and I wanted Averest or Everest. This led to many arguments and to this day I have not even been allowed to name one of our dogs Everest. Jess or Jessica as a name meant a great deal to Pam and her father Mel, so I decided not to challenge a position for which I was vastly outnumbered. I was okay because I was sure that one day I would get to name something Everest (Ten years later I finally accomplished this, and with Pam's support, when I named one of my guitars Averest).

In June we finished building the house, moved in and set about preparing our new home for the bundle of joy growing in Pam. There was no drama during the pregnancy, no big issues at all. Pam was just rock solid and methodical about everything. The day our bundle of joy made her entrance, we knew our lives were going to be changed forever. We would often say to each other: "We just want our baby to be a healthy boy or girl." Even though we didn't know which sex the baby was, everyone I knew thought we were having a boy. The family all knew we were having a boy, the doctor and midwife knew, and I knew: we were having a boy. Looking back on it, I think even everyone on that floor of the hospital knew it too. We were having a boy.

Jessica was born at eight in the evening after 30 hours of labor. When the doctor held her up and announced the birth of my new baby, he said calmly and somewhat comically, "It's a girl." I thought everyone was playing a joke on me, so I took a closer look and by golly sure and shit, it's a girl! Jessica Ann Dana. I shook my head in disbelief: what was I going to do with a little girl? I can't help with girl stuff. I supposed I could play dolls with her, but I was momentarily lost.

Fifteen seconds later the only thing I could see or think about was my daughter.

Jessica was the most beautiful creature in the world to me and I was ready to be Daddy. As the nurses were attending to Jessica they encouraged me to come over and talk to her; she was crying slightly and just a little fussy. As I began to talk softly to her Jessica immediately calmed down and looked at me while I combed her hair. The nurse said she recognized my voice, so I told her I loved her and it was alright because Daddy was there. She stopped crying at that moment and looked up at me, and it was all over for me.

There was my life in front of me, there was my future and when she looked at me with those brilliant blue eyes I could barely control the emotions running through me. While the nurses and doctors attending to Pam were all buzzing around my wife, all I remember is I could not take my eyes off that little baby.

Time was a blur so it could have been just a few minutes or several minutes later, but Pam wanted to hold Jessica. The nurses attending to Pam said she was ready and they handed Jessica to her. Pam asked me to go out and tell the family the good news. I went out to the waiting room, just family were there, and when I told everyone we had a girl I was so overwhelmed I could not control the emotion. I had tears in my eyes and the only thing on my mind was to get back to that baby.

When I got back to Pam and Jessica they were in a new room that had a private quiet room next to it. Pam and the nurses were still talking, so the midwife put Jessica in my arms and guided me to the quiet room where there was a very comfortable rocking chair, low light and just simple, quiet peace. As I was rocking my little girl, holding her tight to my chest, tears just began rolling down my face. I whispered to her over and over again "I promise you, I will always be there for you, you will never be alone and you will never be scared."

I was never going to let her see or experience the things I saw as a child.

Was I a little protective? What do you think? I was so over-the-top protective I am sure I offended more than one person, family member, babysitter or teacher. For any of you that I did offend, please accept my sincere apologies. I really didn't have a lot of control when it came to that instinct.

CHAPTER 14 — THE PRINCESS

Like all new parents, for the first six months of Jessica's life we did not get a lot of sleep, we got tired of diapers and bottles, and both of us started to wonder when would having a kid start to be fun? Throughout this time Pam was nothing but amazing: working full time, cleaning house, taking care of Jessica and keeping me in line.

One summer night — this could perhaps just be what started all of this — Jessica would not fall asleep. Pam was unsuccessful in trying to get her to bed, so I tried several times, also with no success. A few hours later Pam, who was now feeling helpless, pleaded with me to try again to get Jessica to fall asleep. I laid down with Jessica, first on the couch, then the floor. I tried the television and music, and I tried talking to her. Nothing worked. She was crying and fussy and I was running out of options. By two in the morning I didn't think I could take anymore so I decided it was time to load her up in the truck and take her for a drive. She always fell asleep in the car or truck, right? Not this time!

Back at the house I was just about ready to ask Pam to take a turn when I saw our riding lawn mower and thought to myself, "What do I have to lose?" I fired up the loud, obnoxious lawnmower with its loose muffler, put Jessica in my arms and in less than a minute doing slow lazy circles in the driveway she was sound asleep while the noisy engine ran.

Throughout this time Pam and I stayed very active, not really letting baby Jessica slow us down at all. We would boat, camp and travel as long as I felt there was no immediate threat or danger to my family; like I said, I was horribly protective. Truth be told I was always on watch for something, anything that could be a threat; it did not take much and I would remove my family from the situation with haste. This obviously led to more than one embarrassing explanation or apology.

We were so blessed because Pam's parents were close by and completely accessible, and willing to help or give us a break. Wow, did they love their grandbabies. For the first six months after Jessica's birth I felt like I might end up the third wheel, trash man and personal driver. There really was not a lot for me to do but give the kid a bath, change a dirty diaper, give Mom a break and make sure we three were safe and comfortable

At nine months we noticed Jessica was advancing pretty well. She was walking around like it was no big deal and shortly after finding her legs it became clear to Mommy and everyone else that Jessica and I were two peas in a pod. Every chance I could get to fall asleep or take a nap with her I took, every chance she could get to climb in bed with me she took. I actually wanted her to sleep in bed with us and Pam wanted nothing to do with that idea. I would sneak Jessica into bed with us and each and every time she would wake at night I would pull her out of the crib and lay down with her. I was not ever going to let her be afraid at night, like I promised the day she was born.

At 18 months this strategy backfired a little, however.

Lying in bed with Pam one evening about 45 minutes after we put Jessica down for the night in her crib, we heard a loud thud. We were just climbing out of bed, expecting to hear a scream or something, when to our total amazement we heard the pitter-patter of jammy footies sliding over the hardwood floor headed right towards our bedroom. Once Jessica had crawled into bed with us and we could tell nothing was wrong, Pam and I walked to her bedroom and in absolute disbelief we saw a perfectly intact crib. We were expecting the crib to be broken or on its side, but there it stood.

We spent a few minutes with Jessica, telling her it was time to go to bed, and then I carried her back to the crib. Pam and I hid around the corner and waited, and sure enough — Crash! Thud! And then the pitter-patter of small feet. It turned out Jessica was throwing herself over the edge and falling to the floor. It was then we realized we were the three bears, just all in one bed.

For years Jessica would fall asleep with us and after she was sound asleep I carried her into her room and put her into her crib, and when that was a distant memory her big-girl bed. This went on until she got heavy enough that I did not feel like picking her up and carrying her to her own bed.

I am sure there are many of you who are cursing me for allowing Jessica to sleep with us, and I am sure someone will say it scarred her for life. Get over it, I don't care; my promise to her was she would never be scared in bed at night and if it took her being in bed with us, so be it.

By the time she was 2 Jessica and I were always doing something together. I could not imagine not including her in everything we did. Pam, on the other hand, was ready for a break here and there. I didn't care: I was Daddy and I loved it. During this period I had taken over the garage and turned it into a small woodshop so I could build some furniture and a hope chest for Jessica and Pam. As the chest was coming together I would pick Jessica up and put her inside it with a piece of wood while I worked. When I mowed the lawn she was on the mower with me. From time to time I would rent a tractor or bulldozer to work around the property and she would be there with me on them, too. She took any chance there was to ride on something with me.

Yes, we had the Terrible Twos, and yes, we had to discipline Jessica from time to time. I just hated barking at her or swatting her little butt (*with my open hand*), but on very rare occasions this did happen. Pam and I were determined not to raise a little brat, so Jessica never strayed too far from our expectations. She was 3 when she got her last swat on the butt with my open hand. She was raised to be accountable, respectful and confident, just like her mother.

It was when she was 3 or 4 that I realized I could not be happier that I had a little girl. We snuggled constantly and I would try to hug, snuggle and tickle her every day until she could not handle it anymore. We would wrestle at night in bed; "Come on Daddy lets wessel" she would say. I heard that a million times, Pam maybe only a thousand. We would play and play and not once did I ever miss the chance to tell her I loved her. I would always say "Daddy loves you, Princess."

On the few times I had to travel, I always brought back something for her from wherever I was. Beanie Babies were her favorite for the longest time, every airport gift shop had them and it was easy for me. The moment my plane landed I quickly became an unmovable force headed home to see my little girl and wife. Didn't matter what time of night, I would nuzzle up to her and tell her I was home. She usually managed to throw an arm (wet noodle) over my neck and give me a kiss. This was life with my little girl and if this was how it was going to be, I was absolutely content.

CHAPTER 15 — WENDELL

At this point I need to take a step back in time, to late October 1978 — when my family moved to Tenino and I noticed the smoking-hot blonde on the school bus. I met a neighbor named Wendell the same day as I was walking back from the bus stop.

It was about a half-mile from our house to the bus stop along a very well-maintained gravel road lined on each side by tall fir trees. The setting was like being in a park and on this day as I was walking home from the bus stop Wendell stopped in his silver 1978 Chevy pickup and asked me if I wanted a ride to the house. Wendell was just 21 but he had built a house behind the house we lived in and all of his family lived nearby. I said "sure" and hopped in the truck.

For the short ride we exchanged only small talk. He was much older and I was a snot-nosed high school sophomore. When he stopped to let me out at my house, Wendell told me if I ever needed to get out of the house to feel free to just stop by his house and hang out. I was not sure if this was just a friendly neighborly gesture or if he really meant it. For so many years I never really connected with anyone for any duration of time, so I assumed this would be the same.

Wendell knew we spent summers in Alaska and he was mildly interested in talking about Alaska as he was very much an outdoorsman. Wendell had a light-brown beard, long straight hair, the perfect mullet before mullets were in fashion of the same color, and he stood 6 feet and weighted 190. He was not terribly intimidating for his size, but boy did he look the outdoorsman part: part Kenny Rogers and part rodeo cowboy with a little hint of a swamp-water hillbilly. Wendell fancied himself quite the hunter as hunting was deeply rooted in his family's culture. As I would learn later, in the eyes of his family the measure of a man was his ability to kill deer, elk and just about any other warm-blooded creature.

Wendell came from modest means but over the years his family became very successful. His father, who I came to know well, looked and acted a lot like John Wayne. He was a very strong man yet you could tell he cared deeply about his family and kids, and family values. As I got to know Wendell and his father I found them to be very kind but if I made a mistake, said the wrong thing, the bravado and rhetoric would flow. At times it felt like drinking from a fire hose as I had a habit of saying the wrong thing early on.

A couple days after we first met, Wendell stopped by the house to ask me if I hunted. I said I did, but I had had very little experience. This had been one of the big promises Dad made me when motorcycle racing was behind us; we would get to hunt and fish and camp all the time — things I loved to do but it only happened a few times in my 16 years of life. Wendell told me to get my gun and we'd go, so I ran into the house to grab my Sako 30-06.

He looked at my rifle curiously and asked what kind of gun I had as it was pretty fancy for deer hunting. My Dad gave me the rifle for my 14th birthday, although he originally planned to keep it for himself. But one day he learned during a heated conversation at the local bar in Nenana that it was not a good caliber for moose, so he decided to give it to me. Regardless, I treasure that gun to this day.

Wendell and I walked around his father's 80-acre property looking for the elusive and slippery black-tail buck, but we did not see any. We got back to his house right at dark and he said "Hey, are you hungry? Wanna chow?"— he was famous for this saying — and I replied "sure." At this point I did not know why he would even give me the time of day or have even the remotest interest in what my world was like, but I quickly began to admire Wendell and realized he was a real person with a good heart. For some reason he did truly have an interest in my world and our friendship quickly grew.

In almost no time Wendell knew all about the smoking-hot blonde, blue-eyed girl on the school bus and he knew I was smitten to be sure. It was a Friday night, just before elk season, and he asked me if I wanted to go to town and cruise with him. I thought I was going to die: Oh my gosh, I am going to cruise with a guy old enough to buy beer. That would make me so cool the blonde on the school bus would totally think I was cool, too. I asked Wendell to stop by a store so I could buy my girl at home a rose and he thought that was so thoughtful. I wanted Wendell to think I was very mature for my 16 years and I wanted everyone to know about that relationship. I wanted Pam to know how cool I was and wanted everyone at school to know I had a 21 year old in my camp and in all my 16 years I had not ever had a friendship like that.

We stopped at a store and I bought my girl "at home" a rose and we drove to her house to deliver it. Pam in her true fashion said "Oh, thanks" and promptly closed the door, so I turned back to Wendell waiting in the truck and shrugged my shoulders. Oh well, let's hit the road!

That night was amazing: we met girls, he bought beer, we met more girls and he bought more beer. This was the coolest darn thing and just at the point when some of the girls and I started acting stupid and irresponsible, Wendell suddenly cut us off and put an end to the night. On the way home at one in the morning he explained to me that he was okay letting me hang with him, but if I was going to be an idiot or be irresponsible he would prefer we didn't hang out. He reminded me of my girl back home who we delivered the rose to earlier in the evening. I did not know what to make of all this, so I apologized and told him I would try to not act like an idiot in the future. Darn that sucked because he had his own house, lots of bedrooms and I could have been so cool!

Wendell and I spent that winter hunting, fishing, and doing anything we could find for adventure. One day we cut some firewood next to a lake that was frozen over, getting really sweaty and dirty, and he said "Hey, let's jump in the lake." I did not even hesitate and said "sure!" He climbed out of his clothes and dove head first, breaking the quarter of an inch thick ice and swimming out 30 feet. After getting undressed I walked in slowly but slipped and went under. Both of us could barely breathe as we tried to get out of the water, slipping and sliding on the wet clay soil with ice and snow all around. After getting clear of the lake we left the chainsaws in the dirt and jumped into his truck, what we referred to as the 78 Chev, for the 600-yard trip to his house to warm up. He took the back shower and I took the front shower and together we used up all 60 gallons of hot water in five minutes.

Once we were dry and warm, Wendell and I decided it was time go out on the town and chase women (by this time the smoking-hot blonde on the bus had decided it was better not to be tied down to me). There we were, two single guys, mildly wild and full of fun, and oh yeah, by the way we can buy beer. Wendell quickly corrected me, we can buy beer but we don't. That truly made us a hit with the youngsters when we went out cruising, but did not really do much for Wendell and the girls closer to his own age. So when we went out to chase women in the 78 Chev, Wendell would always play the part of older brother/father all wrapped up into one.

One very cold winter night, clear with brilliant stars all over the sky, probably January as I recall, Wendell and I met two girls. They were two very nice girls, but they were interested in Wendell, not me! The gap in our age showed itself big time — can you say awkward? Here I was, riding around with Wendell and two girls who wanted to go drinking and dancing in bars, but I was just 16.

I am sure Wendell would have had the time of his life if he so chose, but instead he offered to take the girls back to his house where he and I would cook them breakfast. Needless to say they were not as interested in breakfast, so after an exchange of phone numbers and small talk we went our separate ways. As I recall Wendell did start dating one of them, I think he had nicknamed her "the ugly one" but that relationship lasted just a short time. To me, this was an early indicator of how Wendell saw and valued relationships with women; a dynamic that impacted every relationship he had.

CHAPTER 16 — I DON'T CARE IF HE IS YOUR BEST FRIEND

By March 1980 it was time to move back to Alaska and I had a girlfriend named Paula, who by the way is still a knock-out today. Well, looking back she was kind of a girlfriend; I think we liked each other but the same old issue got in the way. She knew I was leaving for Alaska and I don't think she was prepared or willing to try to get too close. I also had another newly acquired great friend, Dean, and I had Wendell, who was the best friend I ever had. When Dad told me it was time to drive back to Alaska, he said it would be just him and me. I would get to drive most of the way and when we got there we'd go hunting and fishing. We would be buddies and have a great time.

I still remember the day before I left like it was yesterday. Wendell and I drove around in his $200 Volkswagen Bug, which had no brakes or heater and was set up for off-roading. We were just spending the day together because I think he was disappointed about me leaving as we had become very close. Wendell encouraged me to say goodbye to Dean and Paula, but emotionally I could not do it. In fact, I could barely even stand to be in the car with Wendell; not that I did not want to be there but the emotion of leaving was nearly more than I could take.

As we drove into town to get some gas — 85 cents a gallon back then — we saw Dean and Paula looking for us. They knew I was leaving for Alaska but there was zero chance I would be able to deal with the emotion of spending time with them knowing I was leaving the next morning. At my request Wendell drove off-road and over the hill and through the woods to lose Dean and Paula. To this day I regret that deeply.

After four days of driving 15 hours in ice and snow I was back in Alaska with no phone and no real access to a phone. My only lifeline to "home" was writing letters, and I wrote plenty of them. I wrote to everyone and naturally for a few weeks to a month everyone wrote back to me. Then, because life goes on, the letter count dropped off until there was no more coming to me. I missed Wendell, Dean and Paula and all the other friends I almost connected with in Tenino. I had almost felt like I was one of them and not an outsider.

Then, boom, it happened: Janet! The prettiest girl in Nenana and a senior. I was a junior at this point but this was my first real relationship. If as a young man you have the option to have your first real relationship with a girl like Janet, do it! That's about all I have to say about that! I still think fondly of our numerous trips to the gravel pits, river banks and bonfires.

During one of our rare phone calls over the summer, Wendell told me he was dating a girl named Tami. I thought that was cool, I was dating Janet and maybe we could have a double wedding! In any event Wendell knew how attached I was to Janet, so when our summer affair ended and I was once again headed back "home," he was remarkably thoughtful and warm. He was there to talk, he was there if I needed to eat and he was there if I needed space — he was just great! Wendell and I became sounding boards for each other and our relationships, and although we were terribly competitive, if either of us ever needed anything we knew the other would be there.

A year later Wendell married a gal named Trina in Las Vegas after learning she was pregnant, and they had a son while I was obviously still single and playing the field with school done. We managed to hunt and fish together as often as we could, although time, life and opportunity often took me away from Olympia. By that point tug boating was in my blood and it was a way for me to make good money even though I was traveling all the time.

I was there for Wendell's divorce, which came only a year or so after his son was born, and know how tough it was on him and his very young son. It was also tough on me to travel so much and not be connected to the community and Wendell, so I decided I would follow Wendell's footsteps and build a house in Olympia. The house I planned was a small three-bedroom on five acres; something I thought would connect me to the community and help me find a mate. This was not the case, but it did introduce me to Elena, and my relationship with her forever changed me and led to a turning point in my life, as I am sure Wendell would agree.

A self-proclaimed professional football cheerleader with the looks and body to support that claim, Elena was every man's dream/nightmare come true. A pathological liar, kleptomaniac, party girl, alcoholic, drug user — you name it — with a remarkable ability to cover these traits up as if they did not exist. She was so stunningly attractive, intelligent and charming any warm-blooded man would want to spend time with her. Elena did, however, have one remarkable quality whether sober or impaired, and that I will never forget. But all the rest was a nightmarish blur.

Wendell would often try to convince me Elena was bad news; I on the other hand had taken great interest in her one good quality so I figured all the other issues would eventually become manageable — either that or I did not pay much attention. The relationship ended two days before Christmas 1987 in a parking lot at a gas station in Olympia. I never looked back or second-guessed that decision.

After Pam and I reconnected in the summer of 1988, I called Wendell from Alaska and asked him to stop by my house to check on her. Pam was spending some time at my house after Joe my house sitter had moved out, and I was only a couple weeks from returning to Olympia. He eagerly agreed to do this for me and I told him that she was the girl on Wright Road I was so smitten with some years ago and I was excited to see her again.

Wendell, who was still very single at that time, wasted no time in becoming acquainted with Pam. He even offered to take her quad riding into the mountains to scout for deer or to hang out at his house while he cooked her dinner. Pam shared this with me when I would get a chance to talk to her on the phone and I nearly soiled my pants! Fortunately for me, Pam quickly recognized Wendell for his true perspective on women and she rapidly lost interest in him as anything other than a friend. Thank goodness because being 2,000 miles away I was in an awkward position. Even if he was my best friend I felt somewhat helpless steaming up and down the Yukon River.

During one call Pam asked me if I was sure Wendell was my best friend because he sure seemed like he wanted to date her. I told her that Wendell tried to seduce every tiny blonde blue-eyed girl he met with his wealth and hunting abilities. She laughed and told me that he had done just that but those didn't impress her much and I knew then for sure I wanted to keep this girl.

Wendell was the best man at our wedding and his speech consisted of

"Good luck." That was it, the entire speech! Not a word more! Wendell and I stayed fairly close until his almost-wife Sharon came into the picture and then oh my, did things change. Pam and I knew Sharon and had even spent a small amount of time with her and Wendell, but we both recognized she was on the hunt for money and a sugar daddy. With his tendency to try to use his wealth and hunting skills to impress girls, we knew Wendell had met his match!

Sharon was not good for our friendship and she was not good for Wendell, but all the credit in the world to him he really tried to make things work. During this period Wendell and I could not spend that much time together because of her. Sharon regularly got pregnant right about the time Wendell was getting ready to break up the relationship, and Pam and I told him a hundred times she was trying to get pregnant just for the money. Twenty-one years later she is still looking for money from him and he is still paying child support; I think he has only five more years of support to pay.

Wendell found great joy and relief riding his quad in the hills above his house and became a remarkable rider. He had a Honda TRX 250R and just loved riding and challenging himself and others at the sand dunes. After many conversations about getting an all-terrain vehicle, Wendell finally convinced me that I would love it. I approached Pam and asked her if she would mind me buying a quad so I could ride with Wendell and she said "I don't care what you do with him and I don't care if you buy a quad as long as we can afford it."

I told her there was some great news on that front. Honda had just come out with a TRX 400 that would be faster than his 250, so he and I could spend time together as best friends and wouldn't that be great? Pam paused for a moment and asked me how much this new TRX 400 would cost. I replied, great news on that, it's only $5,800! With that she turned around and as she was walking away I heard her say just loud enough for me to hear: "It is too much money" and "I don't care if he is your best friend."

CHAPTER 17 — WHERE'S MINE, DADDY?

Jessica left the Terrible Twos behind and I very much enjoyed the next couple years with her. She had beautiful, flowing sun-kissed blonde hair and riveting blue eyes that she got from her mother.

She would spend hours riding the battery-powered electric All Terrain Vehicle she received when she was 3 years old. I am pretty sure it was a Christmas present, but it could have been given to her on a birthday. Its mobility was limited to concrete, but nonetheless Jessica had something to ride and it was not all that dangerous, right? It did not take long before she was sliding the rear of the machine around corners and daring the little pink plastic toy to go faster. Pam and I saw this as nothing more than youthful aggression, but even so it was so darn cute to watch. Jessica wore the hard plastic wheels off that toy and eventually it broke.

By this point there was no question Jessica was Daddy's little girl and Pam would often comment that she felt like the stranger in the family. If I went hunting, if I went to the mountains, if I did anything at home or away, there was a pretty good chance Jessica would be with me. She wanted to be with me as much as I wanted her to be there. I always went the extra mile to make sure she was treated like a little girl and she would be comfortable and feel safe. On more than one occasion I had to be bodyguard at the door to a restroom or port-a-potty during our travels.

Pam and I had some rather intense discussions about getting an ATV for me so I could ride with my buddy Wendell, but she finally agreed based on my points that (1) I might lose some weight and (2) she would get a trip to France with her friends. With that agreement, I thought life would be simple.

Boy was I wrong!

I called the Honda dealer, told them what I wanted and said I would be there to pick up the quad in the morning. The next afternoon I had a brand new TRX 400 sitting in the front yard and 30 minutes later I had a brand-new TRX 400 with a broken oil pump. Bugger! I was not going to be riding after all.

Before the breakdown, when the quad was still in the back of the truck, Jessica looked curiously at the ATV then back to me. I could not wait to put her on it to ride with me. But as she walked around the back of the truck, Jessica looked up at me with those blue eyes and asked: "Where's mine, Daddy?"

She was 4-and-a-half at the time, the tiniest thing you ever saw, and her mother gave me a look that said *Don't you even think about it!* I spent 10 minutes trying to convince Jessica that she did not need one because she could ride with me on mine, and we would have so much fun. I put her on the quad with me, we rolled down the driveway and I shifted into second gear so we could cruise at 10 mph slowly back to the house where Mommy was anxiously awaiting the return of her unharmed daughter.

The moment I put her back on the ground Jessica looked up and said "Daddy, I want one too. It's not fair you get one and I don't!" I put Jess back on the ATV with me and took her for another little ride, and she just loved it. I came back, dropped her off with Mom and went back out to test my new toy and its awesome horsepower. Before I got out of second gear the oil pump died and the motor nearly seized up! Hmmmmmmmmmmmmmmm, bugger and maybe a few other choice words was all I could say.

Later that evening Pam, Jessica and I discussed if it would be appropriate to get an ATV for Jessica. Pam asked dozens of questions: Is it safe? How fast will it go? Is she protected? Do they make them that small? *WILL SHE GET HURT*?! I tried to explain to Pam how safe it would be, why it could make sense, how much control I would have, and how at the end of the day it would just be good for the family. Jessica just wanted to be able to ride with her Daddy on her own ATV and I wanted her to have fun together riding like I had with my father on those rare and too few occasions where I had fun with him.

Pam paused a moment and then said, "My dad will kill you if he finds out!" But she reluctantly agreed and the next day we drove down to the Honda dealer and bought a brand-new TRX 90. Jessica's tiny little hands could barely reach the brake levers, those little toes could barely reach the shifter and foot brake, and her thumb could barely reach the throttle. We bought her every piece of safety riding equipment they had: pants, shirt, chest protector, helmet, gloves and boots. Pam saw these purchases and said "You promised me she would not get hurt!" In reply I looked at my wife and knowingly lied through my teeth, promising her Jessica would not get hurt.

Of course, I knew better. Things happen in the blink of an eye and I briefly remembered the wreck where everything changed for me. But I also knew people often got hurt not as a result of their own actions but as a result of the actions or stupidity of others. I simply did not know what to expect from Jessica, but I was going to take every precaution I could think of to keep her safe. I pulled the throttle stop all the way out and bought her what I thought was the best safety equipment. All that was left to do was teach a 4 year old good judgment, how to watch and see everything around her, how to understand closing speed and braking, and — maybe the least important thing — how to drive a 14-horsepower 225-pound machine capable of doing 40 miles per hour.

And Pam was so right about one thing: her dad just blasted me. He said if Jessica got hurt he would hold me completely accountable and he would never forgive me. He tried everything he could to discourage her from riding the ATV, even asking Pam right in front of me if she truly supported the idea or was Troy pushing it down her throat? Mel was ready for a fight if that is what it took to make it clear he objected; he felt it was not something Jessica was interested in but rather my need to live vicariously through Jessica. I think at that moment Pam was not so sure where she stood. I do know it was very difficult for me to look her father in the eye and tell him emphatically that Jessica would not get hurt; I knew better.

Truthfully, I didn't care one tiny bit about having Jessica turn into an ATV riding nut so I could live through her; that was a ridiculous position but I did my best to respect the family's concerns. I truly wanted nothing more than Jessica and I to go explore and take on one adventure after another and it so happened this was a sport I knew well enough that I was mildly confident I could keep her safe. So I told him with absolute sincerity that if — IF! — Jessica did not exercise good judgment, and I meant with no gray areas at all, I would be the first person to pull her off the ATV.

After getting blasted by Pam's entire family for the better part of a month, it may not have appeared to them that I was concerned about my little girl getting hurt. But I did often think of it and that concern and protective instinct never once allowed me to let my guard down when Jessica and I rode together.

I spent hours with her teaching her about hot exhaust pipes, roll overs, brake control, safe zones and danger zones. What was remarkable was my little 4 year old understood what I was telling her just enough to make me feel like we had a chance.

One day that fall, it must have been on a weekend, I decided we would spend the day, if she could handle it, teaching Jessica how to ride. We started with me riding on back with her, my hands on the handlebars and throttle as she went through the motions while we putted around the yard. Each time we made a loop or turned a different direction I could feel her arms on the handlebars, putting pressure in the direction her eyes wanted to go. I was so content to be in that moment and she had no idea that we were doing anything more than just riding.

We did this for some time, maybe 15 minutes, and then I gave her control of the throttle. Jessica had exceptional control of the throttle and she instantly understood her speed was relative to her thumb input. Of course this throttle control came after a few abrupt accelerations and her helmet hitting me square in the jaw. My jaw and nose were bruised and discolored by the end of that lesson but I didn't care one bit; I was in heaven.

I spent several days over the next couple of months, basically whenever the weather would permit, riding with Jessica on her ATV until I was sure she could handle it on her own. She was nearly 5 by the time I let her ride without me on the seat behind her. She got on the ATV by herself and took off with a confidence that grew each time.

At this time we started talking about taking a trip to the sand dunes in Oregon, driving down there for a few days of camping and riding. A trip that would be too good to be true for a proud Daddy! To prepare Jessica I had her follow my 400 with her 90 as I led her places on our own property where I knew she would have some fear. I did this to show her how she could use me and my ATV to stop and turn as well as building her confidence and skills, and my comfort with her judgment.

When I decided she was ready, we decided to head to the dunes the first week of February 1999. Wendell and I had planned the trip: he would bring his nephew and two daughters, Nichole and Morgan, and I would bring my nephew Ferris and Jessica. We would camp on the sand, ride until we got sick of riding — and then ride some more.

The weather forecast looked perfect, and just when I thought life would be simple Pam objected to the trip, citing danger, Jess was too young and my inability to protect Jess from any and every conceivable threat or danger. My solution was to have Pam go, but Pam said she was not going: no way, no how, not happening. She was pissed when I told her Jessica and I would go anyway. She blasted me 20 times, then I was blasted by her parents, and then again by my father. Everyone was convinced Jessica would be hurt: she was just too young, and I was only thinking about myself.

When we arrived at the dunes for the first time Jessica and I were amazed at how big an area it was and how little we were in comparison. We parked our little camp trailer in the sand with pine trees surrounding us on three sides. After unloading the quads and setting up camp we were excited to go ride. Initially, Jessica did not want to ride her own ATV and she preferred and was content to ride on my ATV with me. It didn't take long however and after a few trips around the camp area she was ready to ride her own quad. After that she asked me every chance she could to start her ATV so she could ride. I made sure she knew she must stay close in to our camp so I could see her every moment. Jessica made her own little trail in the sand between the trees and around camp and must have done 200 laps on it; I watched intently all 200 laps and she knew without question I was staring at her every moment.

I had the time of my life on that trip; I beamed with pride and my cheek bones were sore from smiling from ear to ear. We rode day and night, on hills and trails on the beach. At night we sat by the fire in our camp eating awesome camp food and just had an amazing time. Of course I was so sore I could barely walk or stand up the morning of our return.

Wendell commented numerous times how much he enjoyed this type of camping and riding with the kids, and Jessica and I became even closer, if that was possible. Sitting by the fire the last night before leaving the dunes to return home, with the cool ocean air blowing lightly through the camp, Wendell and I agreed we would try to return three or four times a year.

CHAPTER 18 — SHE WON A TROPHY

By the time Jessica turned 8 in the summer of 2002, she was a wily veteran of ATV riding. This was in large part because of the six or seven trips she made to the Oregon dunes to ride, camp, play, laugh and just enjoy being a kid — and lucky for me she hadn't even gotten a bruise yet!

Around this time I heard about an event in southern Oregon called Dune Fest, including that it was a great experience but also how wild and dangerous it could be. By now Pam was feeling a little better about the dangers of ATV riding and was getting more comfortable with the sport, so she decided to go with us to Dune Fest and experience the event and be part of what Jessica and I had developed a passion for. While I was telling Jessica what I knew about Dune Fest, I also told her Mommy was coming with us. Jessica walked over to me, flopped in my lap and looked up with those big blue eyes to ask: "Does she really have to go?" I thought I was going to die, but I told her "Yes, Mommy has to go." Cousin Ferris was also going and we were going to be meeting some other friends there.

Like the first time going to any big event, conference or destination, our first trip to Dune Fest was all about learning: learning where we could and couldn't tow our heavy trailer in the sand, and where services were and were not. You get the point, and for our inaugural Dune Fest we made every wrong decision. We ended up parking miles from events, far from anything actually, and we parked in the worst soft sand possible. All in all Pam's first personal experience with the sport was not good. We had 300-foot-tall sand dunes all around and above us, and ATVs screaming past our camp at 90 miles per hour. No, Pam was not impressed or comfortable — at all.

On one of our rides around the massive dune riding area to see what was going on, we noticed a drag strip had been set up with a professional drag tree — an electronic starting device with yellow, green and red lights — two well-groomed lanes and a nice run-out area. I asked Jessica if she wanted to drag race and she said "sure" even though she had no idea what it was.

The sand was dry and soft and the owner was doing some testing so we got to watch 20 or so test passes with quads staging — getting right on the starting line — and using the drag tree. Pam reluctantly agreed to let Jessica race after several minutes of negotiation, so I entered her into the kids 5-16 years old class.

Jessica was given two practice runs so we could bracket her, or determine her handicap by establishing a predicted elapsed time for a run which allows racers with different equipment to compete against each other. The competition itself was single elimination: lose and you're done, win and you move on to the next round.

While we were waiting our turn, Jessica suddenly turned to me, nearly knocking me over with the bill of her helmet, and said: "Daddy, give me a hug!" Never one to turn down a hug with my daughter, I snuggled with Jessica and went over what she needed to do to make a pass. I reminded her to move slowly into the staging area and to stop when she saw the two yellow lights on top. Next the yellow lights would start to move down the drag tree, and when she saw the green ones it was time to GO! I told her to hold the throttle wide open and the handlebars straight until the end of the pass, and then to come back to the pits.

We watched other riders make passes and I asked, "See how those guys are doing it?" There were also folks on the track to help the kids go the right way. Two practice runs later I gave the track official her dial-in time thinking I could use the fact that she was slower to our advantage. We were dialed-in and ready for whatever the track was going to give us. It was windy and a little chilly, but for me it was a great day because I had my little girl and my wife, and we were enjoying the moment.

Ferris, who by this time had become an exceptional talent on a quad, was also racing. His turn came up first, and at the green light he nailed the throttle, sending sand flying from his rear tires eight feet in the air and 30 feet behind the quad. Ferris didn't quite understand the principle of drag racing was to go fast from start to finish for 300 feet in the sand consistently. He rather thought it would be just as important to look cool and try to go fast. Much to his utter and complete disappointment he ended up doing wheelies down the lane and was eliminated after one pass. Apparently the hour or so of coaching and strategy I discussed with him didn't stick.

When it was Jessica's turn she needed a little help from the starter to get staged, but she left right on the green light and ended up winning her round because the other racer broke out — went faster than his handicap time. Jessica did exactly what I asked her to do and it worked. Pam and I were shocked but happy to be heading to the second round where Jess was paired up with a comparable quad. Ferris was angry beyond belief and wouldn't even watch Jessica move to the next round. And what do you know? She stunned us all by winning again. On her third pass the other rider's quad broke down, giving her the win, and the round after that her competitor, an older kid on an ATV twice as fast as Jessica's, tripped the red lights by leaving too early.

That put Jessica in the finals where she lined up against a 16-year-old girl on a 500cc ATV with an automatic transmission. For comparison, Jess had a 90cc ATV with a four-speed transmission. We kind of knew the outcome of the final round before it even started: Jessica's manual transmission would be a real disadvantage. But by now Jessica was showing signs of understanding competition and she said she wanted to beat that girl. Mommy was beaming from the pits, and I told her how proud I was and how much I loved her, and to just go have fun. Don't get me wrong, I wanted Jessica to beat this girl too, but we also knew an 8 year old and 12 hp was no match for a 16 year old and 45 hp!

Jessica rolled up to the staging lights and I let her do it on her own, with no help at all. Once she was staged, the other girl rolled in and staged on the start line. Jessica was to leave first because of the bracket offset, and when she saw the green light she nailed the throttle and — the ATV died! She turned around to look back at me and put her arms out as if to say *what do I do?* I ran to her as quickly as I could through the sand, but the 16-year-old girl had already made her pass and won the race.

After running the 50 feet or so in the soft sand up to her and starting the ATV, I told her it was okay and to just go finish the race. I patted her on the head and off she went. She placed second, getting a trophy nearly as tall as she was, but more importantly for this story she now had a taste for competition.

On the other hand, after seeing that trophy Ferris was green with envy. The poor kid was dying inside over that trophy and to this day he still holds a grudge.

CHAPTER 19 — DADDY, I NEED MORE HORSEPOWER!

By December 2003 it became pretty clear to Pam and I that Jessica had out-grown the 90 ATV. Even though she was only 8 she was riding my 400, with several thousand dollars of go-fast parts on and in it, with absolute confidence and good judgment. On trips to the dunes she would drag race adult men and others on very fast ATVs and beat them run after run. Wendell and Jessica would drag race for a half-hour straight and Jessica would just stomp him pass after pass. She was going much faster on my hopped-up 400, too, pushing 65-70 miles per hour.

Jessica looked so tiny on my ATV that it never failed to catch people's attention wherever we went. Riders would notice the blonde hair and then realize she was just a little girl. But when it was time to race, she was just another racer to these guys — and pretty darn good to boot. Before she would line up for any race I would evaluate the racer, sand conditions and wind direction, and if for a second I did not feel she was safe I would pull her out or tell her to line up differently. At that speed it was not uncommon to have tire-to-tire contact and one rider would get catapulted into the air 10-15 feet at 70 mph; I was not ready to see that.

As she improved Jessica lost all interest in riding her 90, and while commonsense may have been to let her grow more in size, I was comfortable with moving her up to the next step. I negotiated the trade-in of the 90 for a brand-new TRX 300 and planned to get one for Mommy, too, as she was now showing more interest in going to the sand dunes, camping and being together.

Pam and Wendell never did really hit it off — actually as she came to know him better she found his views that women were for making babies, cooking and cleaning house to be offensive, as did the majority of his girl friends over the years — but she was always comfortable with him and the kids in the riding environment. Pam also knew Jessica was always safe around him, and she trusted Wendell's judgment when it came to Jessica and her riding ability. Even Wendell told Pam that Jessica could handle the next level. We all agreed: Jessica was ready for the next step.

I made arrangements to have Santa leave the new ATV at Nana's and Papa's house for Christmas. I wanted to see the joy on her face after getting an ATV from Santa; she still "believed" at that point and we were so darn proud of that fact. Every year when Christmas morning came we made a point, regardless of where we were to celebrate the holiday, that Santa would visit our house, too. One winter in particular I made reindeer hoof prints in the gravel for Jessica to see because she began to question if a bunch of reindeer and a short fat man with presents could land on our roof. This was a simple fact of life for our family: Jessica woke up on Christmas knowing Santa had been there for her.

For this, however, I decided the entire family should get to see her reaction when she saw the new 300. But, Nana and Papa were hardly amused when, a couple days before Christmas, I delivered it to their house, which is where we would celebrate that year.

Christmas morning after Santa visited our house, we went over to Nana and Papa's to spend the holiday with the entire family. This too was a family tradition that Jessica had known as long as she'd been alive. When the time came for opening presents, Jessica found her new 300 from Santa but she showed mild enthusiasm; Jessica knew how little her grandparents liked quads and she immediately noticed the reaction from the family was lukewarm at best. None of Pam's family and only a couple folks from my side had any interest in seeing Jessica riding a quad or — even worse — compete on one.

Holidays with Pam's family were nothing like anything I ever experienced as a kid or young adult with my family. Her entire family spent the day laughing, sharing, eating and being together — such an amazing experience for me. But this particular Christmas had a little bit of a cloud over it because of the quad.

When it came time to take the presents and Jessica's shiny new ATV home at the end of the day, I got some help putting the polarizing Christmas present into the back of the truck. I left to make the four-mile or so run to our house just before dark and just as I got to the top of the hill and our driveway the quad rolled out the back of the truck and bounced off the ground six feet in the air! After a few more bounces it occurred to me that I had forgotten to tie it down, in the process doing a couple thousand dollars in damage to Jessica's Christmas present.

I still hear about that from time to time, believe me.

At the same time, I bought Pam a TRX 300 to help her feel more connected to us when we went riding. Pam wanted to be a part of what Jessica and I were doing, and to be more than just the camp cook. Pam could see the simple joy in Jessica's eyes whenever she came home and told Mommy about our trips to the dunes, the funny things that happened or something interesting. Pam wanted to ride but it did not take long to figure out that if Jessica had her mother's natural talent for riding ATVs there is no doubt in my mind my daughter would have gotten hurt and hurt bad! Pam was not a natural and that really took the fun out of riding for her.

Buying the two 300s for Jess and Pam proved to be a bad investment. Jessica rode her 300 once, got off and hopped back on my 400. The 300 just did not have enough power according to Jessica, my 9-year-old little girl. Pam also had distaste for her 300, citing a lack of power as well, but I think Pam just overheard Jessica and went along. At any rate, the 300s lasted one trip before I found myself back at the Honda shop to buy two new 400s, one for Pam and one for Jessica. The 400s were shiny, brand-new Hondas, painted bright red, and they were a hit with Pam and Jessica.

We went back to Dune Fest the next year and even though Jessica was just 9, I got the okay from the race director for her to race my very fast 400. She put down some low 5-second passes and amazed the crowd so much that each time she staged at the drag tree 500-700 people would stand up and applaud. The race director told me later that day that she was the fastest 9 year old in the country as far as he knew, and that he had never seen a little girl so naturally talented.

Jessica quickly became very popular at Dune Fest, and Pam and I were typical beaming parents. She was still my little girl, though, so we gave each other random hugs anytime and anywhere in the pits. People would look at the three of us and the tight family bond and smile at the sight.

In no time at all Jessica had outgrown her 400. At the tender age of 10 she could ride with our group, climb hills and, oh my, could she drag race. By this time I had purchased a 450 and pumped it up so it was one bad-fast ATV, and Jessica just had to have one, too. Rather than try another Christmas present, Pam and I went down on Valentine's Day and bought her a brand-new 450 of her own. Pam had transitioned from being patently negative and obstructive to supportive and incrementally more confident in Jessica and her abilities.

Around this time Pam started losing interest in going with us to the dunes. This was partly because Wendell always went and partly because she was pretty much camp cook, meaning it was a lot of work for her. Occasionally, I could get her to ride with me and we always tried to catch sunsets on the beach. Once the sun went down we returned to camp to enjoy the fire, eat some great camp food and laugh about all the crazy things our group had done that day.

On a trip in 2005 to Sand Lakes on the Oregon coast, Pam, the kids and I watched the sunset together and then we went to do some drag racing up the hills off the beach. Ferris and I were racing neck-and-neck at about 50 mile per hour when we made hard contact — very hard contact. My tire went flat and that drove me into Ferris at full-throttle, launching me off my ATV. I flew about 25 feet up hill and landed on my right shoulder and back. Ferris somehow stayed with his ATV but when it stopped he was hanging over the front fender looking directly into the headlight. He was okay, but I was not doing too well and Pam and Jessica were very shook up after watching the crash from the beach.

Pam saw lights flying through the air and sand flying 20 feet high and then nothing, all dark. She and Jessica rode up as fast as they could to find me lying still with no air in my lungs. I could tell I was hurt but I did not want to upset them, so I took it easy for the rest of the trip. After several months of misery I found out I had a fracture in my back and having Jessica walk on my back every night was not a particularly wise treatment option.

From 2005 to 2008 I also got to enjoy the privilege of having a few of

Jessica's friends join us for trips to the sand dunes. I considered it a great responsibility and privilege for her friend's parents to allow their daughters go with us to the dunes to ride, camp and have fun. To have those parents trust me with their children while taking part in an inherently dangerous sport in a particularly dangerous environment was an honor to me.

Several of these trips included Maleah, the daughter of Paul and Senna and Jessica's best friend throughout much of her grade- and middle-school years. Pam and I felt like Maleah was our second daughter, but we also got to know and love Paul and Senna.

Handsome, confident and just over 6-foot, a man's man in every way, Paul is the kind of guy who everyone wants to be around and no one wants to mess with. Senna is just over 5-foot, with dark brown flowing hair and the looks and figure of a Greek goddess; Senna could stop traffic on a freeway with her stunning looks, but she is also the most pleasant and authentically humble beautiful woman we have ever come to know.

Pam and I consider ourselves very lucky to have the privilege of saying we are good friends with Paul and Senna, and to this day we enjoy spending time with them, going out to dinner and enjoying each other's company. Like clockwork each time the four of us would go to dinner or a function we laughed so hard our stomachs would be sore by the end of the evening.

CHAPTER 20 — DUNE FEST 2008

In 2006 and 2007 we managed to make several trips to Oregon to ride at the dunes and Jessica continued to improve her riding skills. She would rarely pass up an opportunity to drag race someone at the dunes but when it came to entering the drags at Dune Fest, she just didn't have the desire. By contrast I had the bug: I knew she could kick ass and with her tiny 110-pound frame we had a built-in advantage on even the best riders.

By 2008, Jessica and I had made many trips to the Oregon dunes to ride and ride and ride, as well as several trips to Dune Fest. Mom decided she didn't want to go to the dunes anymore because the speeds and danger had gone way up in her mind, and at the end of the day it was just not her cup of tea

For those three years I got us ready for Dune Fest, preparing Jessica's quad for drag racing plus mine just in case she wanted to compete. Three years in a row once we got there she would say she was not all that interested in the actual competition. My sense was she felt that way because it was not as easy to win as it had been before. The other riders she faced were better and I had to work harder than ever to keep her competitive; we were always racing one and two classes over her head along with racing in the age-appropriate classes.

I even put her on my blazing-fast 450 to make her more confident she could compete, but there just was no desire there. Jessica just did not show any interest from her amazing runs at the ages of 8 and 9. Privately, I hoped she would find interest in it again, but at that time it simply was not there so if it wasn't meant to be, it just wasn't meant to be. I was disappointed and frustrated because I could sense she wanted to compete but she didn't want to deal with not performing well if that is what happened. I told her as long as she tried her hardest I wouldn't care if we got first or last, just to try her best.

In several ways, life had changed for the three of us that summer. First, Jessica seemed to have just grown up overnight. Secondly, it changed because I saw and knew just how talented she could be as a drag racer. And finally, it changed because about six months earlier we sold my real estate company to one of the largest commercial real estate firms in the world, and that turned out to be a financial disaster for our family. Like I said, this story is not about me but there is no doubt Jessica was impacted by this event and the fall-out: we lost not only our income but our retirement and ability to make money for just over a year and a half.

By this time Wendell had become a very successful single man, not by choice mind you, but because he was never able to wisely choose a potential wife. On those rare occasions where he did pick good women he usually failed to develop healthy relationships based on mutual respect with them. He had a sort of "me man, you woman" approach to his relationships. Pam tolerated his often-sexist and disrespectful statements about women as if they were all the same creature, but she no longer had any interest in attending Dune Fest with us.

By early summer Wendell, in his usual fashion, could not decide if he wanted to go to Dune Fest. He always had too much to do, too much to load, it would take too long to load up the equipment, it would be too expensive and all we would do is hang around the drag strip and eat food. This was classic Wendell: no matter what you were going to do, he was going to complain and drag his feet. If you were headed to Disneyland, he would complain about the music and mouse ears. I finally told him I was going with or without him, and that prompted him to talk to his two daughters and they naturally said they wanted to go.

By delaying the decision to attend Dune Fest we ended up with a less than desirable camp site, but Wendell and I decided to take the girls and have a couple of the boys who worked for us from time to time meet us down there. We would ride and maybe try the drag strip as Wendell's oldest daughter Nichole was interested in drag racing. I did not have much hope Jessica would want to race so I did not push it with her too hard, but just in case I had my 450 dialed-in.

Jessica said: "Nope, Daddy, I don't want to drag race, I just want to ride and have fun … you're just going to have to have a son if you want a racer."

There it was, I had been told, end of story.

The weather that year was hit-and-miss: rain in the morning and cool and overcast in the afternoon for the first couple days, then the sun came back for the last two days of the event. So I was not all that heartbroken, but boy did I want to see that kid make a few passes on my scary-fast 450.

When it was time for the first race, High School Drags, Wendell and Nichole headed to the strip with her 400 while Jessica and I stayed back at the trailer. Jessica was still too young to let her ride alone and we decided to wait for Wendell and Nichole to come back from the strip and then go for a long ride as a group. An hour later Nichole and Wendell came back and Nichole was holding a big trophy, second place in the High School Drags. Nichole was 16 at the time and was by all accounts a very good drag racer, not overly-talented as an all-around driver but she could concentrate and follow instructions.

That trophy was like a slap in the face and wake-up call to Jessica, who was envious but also happy for Nichole. They were as close as sisters in many respects, having growing up together. Wendell was beaming because Nichole was able to beat dozens of faster and more powerful ATVs on a stock 400.

Not about to be upstaged by the trophy being displayed proudly by Nichole, Jessica pulled me aside to ask if I thought she too could win a trophy. I replied the only chance was to give it a try. As we were mulling our options for what ATV Jessica would drive in the next day's event, she asked me if she could win on the four-wheel drive ATV rather than run either of our fast 450s. I told her it was possible; she would be going only 31 miles per hour but drag races are won by consistency. We decided she had a better chance of winning on the four-wheel-drive ATV with an automatic transmission. I was disappointed but refused to let it show as I was also excited she found her will to compete. I was just not sure I could coach her or do much to the machine to help her; all I could tell her was to cut a good light and hit the throttle.

We woke up the next morning to a miserable cold rain, but Jessica was excited to get to the drag strip so we promptly filled the gas tank on the four-wheel drive ATV. The plan was to run full-throttle on each pass for consistency and I dropped the air pressure all the way around to 1.5 pounds for traction. After that there was nothing for me to do except remind Jessica to watch the tree and get the rhythm of the lights down, like Nichole had done, so she could get a good start. The day before Nichole's reaction time from green light to take off was .41 seconds; that was as good as 15-time National Hot Rod Association (NHRA) champion John Force could do.

It was raining hard, we were cold and wet, and I was standing beside Jessica in wet, heavy sand as the other ATVs rolled up to take the first of two allowed practice runs before eliminations began. Sitting on the four-wheel drive ATV, Jessica was soaked and shivering in her tiny sweatshirt and her attitude was rapidly deteriorating. She was at that age where she was keenly concerned about how she was dressed, regardless of how cold the weather was. I was standing next to her wearing a cotton coat with a T-shirt underneath it and I was also cold — but not as miserable as Jessica.

We were about 15 minutes from making our first pass and Jessica decided she had had enough — she was not going to race. This for her just was not fun. Frustrated, I told her in a very firm tone that "Winner's race." Mad at me for what I said, she looked down for a moment and then looked back at me. She said: "Go get my 450 and give me your coat then." I was never more proud or happy as I was that day standing in the freezing-cold rain without a coat.

We only had a few minutes to get her lined-up and get her 450 to the pits, but one of the boys happened to be nearby and he ran to get Jessica's ATV. I was a little angry because I did not have any time to prepare her 450: air pressure, fuel, gearing, tire selection, nothing! My role was to make sure she had the best possible set-up I could give her with my very limited knowledge and understanding, now it would be all her without any of my tuning.

I tested the rear tires with my hands, yup, there's air in them but I had no idea how much. This would be critical because we needed two good, solid passes to pick a dial-in time. Unequal air pressure will pull the machine either left or right under full power acceleration.

Prior to this race I always told Jessica to hold the throttle about half open, but this day my instruction to her was to just hold it wide open. Surprised at that she said: "WHAT?!" I told her the motor would hit the protecting rev-limit chip, but if it did blow up I would get it fixed. I smiled at her, tapped her on the helmet and said "Go give 'em hell!"

Jessica launched her 450 on the first practice run and the sand was so heavy it only flew up about six feet. That was okay because it just made her mad and more determined; I could deal with that. The second test pass she rolled off on a near-perfect start and put down a super pass, the problem was it was three-tenths faster than the first pass. Now we're screwed! After a brief lecture about waiting to the last second to make the right choice, how hard it made things on me, and showing her the times, we looked at each other and said "I guess we will just have to figure it out" at almost the exact same time.

Eliminations were next on the schedule and Nichole made her first pass and won. Jessica was a little nervous, knowing we were flying blind and that I could not change anything for her. She rolled into the staging lane, triggering first one and then both yellow lights. Her competitor staged, the tree lit up with all yellows and then green. The 450 was bouncing off the rev chip at 11,500 revolutions per minute and she exploded off the line, shifted up to second gear and lifted the front tires off the ground a few inches. Jessica hit third gear and then fourth and she was across the finish line with a nice, easy roll-out. The flashing light was on in Jessica's lane — she won!

Now with a little more confidence, we had a few minutes to talk before the next race. I studied the race print-out listing Jessica's pass time, speed, dial-in time, reaction time, and sixty-foot time. The strip was 300 feet of wet sand and when the rain stopped it got softer and softer throughout the day. Jessica was driving better than we expected and I noticed she was way too close to dial-in time and in danger of breaking out. We needed her to slow down a little but races are often won or lost by tenths of a second, so for the next race I suggested Jessica tap the brake just before the finish line if she was leading. Jessica had a much better idea and said "What if I just pull in the clutch?" I smiled wide and told her that was it, pull in the clutch if you are ahead but don't let them beat you over the line.

For the second elimination race she was the slower ATV by bracket time, so Jessica left the line first and the faster rider had 300 feet to run her down for the win. Even with the sand getting softer, Jessica was driving better and better, and she beat him to the line and pulled in the clutch. The little bugger had done it again — we got the flashing light. Nichole also won her race and Wendell and I were so darn excited we would have been content if that was all the further either girl went.

Jessica drew the fastest ATV with the best rider in the class for the third race of eliminations. Brutally consistent and with confidence oozing out of him, this rider was on a YFZ 450. Honda 450s are prone to wheelies on launch due to a higher center of gravity but the YFZ 450 did not suffer from this tendency that impacted speed, time and consistency. We were already dangerously close to breaking out of bracket because our dial-in time was just a tad slow while Jessica was getting faster as the day wore on. Jessica and I knew this would be her toughest race and Wendell came over to talk to us as his daughter Nichole had also drawn a very competitive rider.

As we sat in the pits pondering our race strategy, I said "Run all out, that is the only way we can beat this kid." We would lose if we broke out or if he beat her in the first 60 feet, so our only chance was to go for broke. If Jessica won she would advance to the trophy round, a loss and she would be done and in fifth place.

By that time the sun was starting to dry the sand more and the wind was negligible, conditions that favored the better rider. When called to the lane and told to roll out, Jessica drew the right lane and the fast kid was on the left. Just before she rolled out I said to Jessica, smiling ear to ear: "Give it all you got!" Trying to work on his nerves she let him stage first but it did not work; this kid was good and he was not terribly worried about a little 13-year-old girl giving him the run of his life.

Jessica rolled up and staged, one yellow, two yellows, and the tree began its drop to green. Jessica launched with the throttle wide open while the third yellow light was completely lit and my heart sank for a moment before I noticed we were still green! Sand came up behind the rear tires 12 feet in the air and at 30 feet Jessica was already in second gear with the front tires off the ground about 8 inches and she did not even burp the throttle. I watched the fast kid on the 450 and listened to Jessica as she shifted, knowing she needed a prefect run and to not break-out. Second gear, 11,500 rpm, third gear 11,500 rpm and it was all over in 5.5 seconds. Jessica won the race to the line and avoided breaking out by .003 of a second. I asked her for her best drive and she gave it to me. We nearly squeezed the air out of each other when she returned to the pits.

Nichole also had her best run and there we were: Jessica and Nichole had survived eliminations and were in the top three. As Jessica came back to settle into the pits she pulled over to watch Nichole run for a place in the final round. Nichole cut another near-perfect .411 light to secure her place in the final round racing against Jessica for first. Wendell and I were both just on cloud nine; we could not believe how fun this was and how great the girls were driving. It was amazing to be able to take two young girls with limited racing experience and see them perform so well.

For the final round Jessica lined up in the right lane and Nichole was in the left. Jessica had the faster ATV by .50 seconds so Nichole would launch first, an added challenge for Jessica. She had five seconds to have a perfect light, chase Nicole down and pass her, and then slow down enough to not break-out of her dial-in time. But once again, when she needed to perform her best, Jessica did exactly as I asked her to.

She was able to win the race for first place and Nichole was right there as the runner-up. Wendell and I could not have been more proud or excited. We were both very engaged fathers enjoying this once in a lifetime opportunity to be with our daughters and watch them compete and win races that they probably shouldn't.

It was at this time Jessica developed the competitive look in her eye that today has become only more intense. When she got back to the pits and realized she won, Jessica nearly knocked me down giving me a hug. We must have squeezed each other for a full minute and I was fighting back tears realizing how much this would do for her confidence. She knew she had second place for sure if she just finished, but she wanted to win and she wanted to hold up that winner's trophy.

Jessica would go on to compete in a total of six events that weekend, winning the Index class, placing third in two events and top-10 in two more. Nichole finished in second place two more times so during the trophy presentation at the end of the event our girls walked to the stage five times.

That night was our last at Dune Fest and Wendell and I took our ATVs out for one last ride before it got dark. We rode hard, climbed monster hills, took massive jumps and played like we were 16-year-old boys on brand-new machines without a care in the world. We laughed at everything we did, even if it was not remotely funny. Of all the people in the world, Wendell is the one guy I would have wanted this to happen with and it goes down as one of the many memories he and I have to take with us.

CHAPTER 21 — "GO KARTS?" TO NATIONALS IN JUST WEEKS

In August 2009 we were enjoying all that summer in the Pacific Northwest had to offer when Jessica asked me to take her to the local race track, South Sound Speedway in Tenino, Washington. We went to watch the race, but the sounds, speed of the cars and smells of racing fuel and burnt rubber seemed to affect her. She started asking me questions: How fast were the various classes of car? How hard to drive were they? Could she try to drive a race car?

Throughout her entire life I had tried to let her do and try everything she was interested in, within reason. Her mother, however, I knew was not going to see this as an opportunity but instead as nothing more than a great big mistake. Jessica was very good on ATVs and she could drive our tractor all around our property, but drive a race car? I asked a friend about letting Jessica take some laps in his two-third scale race car at the speedway. He was great and said "No problem, but you wreck it, you buy it," and he suggested I take her to get some laps in a go-kart first.

I took her to our local indoor track, Apex Karting, which as of the time of this writing is regrettably no longer in business due to the economy. Jessica and I entered the facility and found it was well-run, with very nice equipment. We also noticed there was a way to track your speed and times compared to the others racing at the facility; a very cool computer screen captured the racing live and displayed race results and rankings. You also received a print-out to take home at the end of each race, and we thought that was pretty cool. I purchased a few races for Jessica and she, being a little shy and timid, was not going out to drive the kart unless I was out there with her. So Daddy was now a kart driver as well and together we drove three or four races at the track.

It was clear to me and anyone who watched her that Jessica was pretty good without ever having any prior experience in a kart. The track owner noticed the same thing and mentioned to me that Mike Smith, the reigning national indoor karting champion, would be at the facility the following week. He thought it would be interesting to have Mike see Jessica drive. At this point my focus was still simply getting Jessica into a race car and karting seemed to me more like an amusement park ride.

I would learn later how remarkably wrong I was about that, and just how much talent was required to drive an indoor kart fast.

When Mike Smith watched Jessica make laps at Apex he instantly recognized she had some natural talent, but he told me her overall lack of racing experience was something that may work against her. In any event, Mike and Jessica quickly became good friends, the teacher and the student, and I came to consider him to be one of the most gifted and knowledgeable racers I have ever seen.

In addition to winning the national indoor championship in 2008, Mike raced karts in Europe and all over the United States. A fit man just shy of 6-foot tall and 185 pounds, Mike has blonde hair and an infectious personality that made him liked by everyone at the track. He is also a fierce competitor with a love of the sport he has been so closely connected with, making him one of the best advocates karting could ever have. It is only a matter of time before Mike plays a role in the development of another great young talent.

Jessica and I quickly became "regulars" at Apex Karting, often making the trip there to practice and get laps. At the same time I made arrangements for Jessica to drive my friend's two-thirds scale race car, called a Baby Grand, with the idea of possibly buying it. Testing at South Sound Speedway did not prove much as Jessica was so new to the car and that style of racing. But, she wanted to try and we allowed her to enter one race late in August 2009. In the end the plan to ease into asphalt-track car racing with the Baby Grand was put on hold because I had extreme reservations about the class of car and expense involved.

We decided to focus on karting instead, and by September Jessica had become a popular and respected regular at Apex Karting, often running lap times in the top one percent of the fastest drivers there. Mike Smith took me aside one day and asked if I would be open to Jessica competing in the upcoming Indoor National Karting Championships in Phoenix, Arizona. We had experienced and seen firsthand how quickly Jessica became one of the top-10 ranked drivers at Apex in just twelve weeks, but her mother and I were skeptical she truly had the talent to compete at that level.

We discussed the opportunity as a family, weighing the cost and the commitment for practice that Mike would require of her and our family. Together, we decided to give it a try; if nothing else we would get to see Arizona in November. Jessica practiced every chance she could during the six weeks leading up to the event, including spending Sunday mornings at Apex. Even with that, when the day came to head to the airport for the flight south Mike and I knew that because of Jessica's lack of experience she simply may not be competitive in Phoenix. As a sport, we learned karting is deceptive. It is physically demanding and to excel a driver needs uncanny focus, vision and skills.

In addition to acting as our team manager, Mike would be competing to defend his title. That meant Daddy was going to be Jessica's spotter and chief strategist, something that was not the first choice of either of us. My experience with the sport was as limited as hers, with the important exception that she was much more talented behind the wheel than I was with a radio.

Our first day at F1 Racing in Phoenix was for practice, but try as we might Jessica was a full second slower than everyone on the track. All drivers were required to run at a race weight of 200 pounds, which meant Jessica had to add a great deal of lead ballast to her kart. Mike had very little time to work with us, so he suggested running Jessica at race weight and seeing what happened. If she was not competitive, so be it — we had no expectations and she would enjoy the experience.

What Mike did not know then is that neither Jessica nor I attended competitive events to *NOT* be competitive.

Jessica's frustration was sky high, she did not like being so far off race pace and she knew if we didn't find the pace we would not be competitive. I was determined to figure out how I could make her faster; she had the basic skill-set and knowledge; what I needed to work on was her confidence. First I decided to have her run laps without the extra added weight to see if she could find the pace. It worked and she laid down lap times comparable to the ten fastest drivers.

Now knowing she could run fast laps without the required extra weight, I tricked her into believing she was at the right weight because that was how Mike wanted her to practice. If Mike had told her she needed to chew on a snail while racing she would have done it. We were only a second off pace and I was confident we could find that second by bringing back the 70 pounds on the kart. Sure enough, it worked and I could see her confidence grow. I began to slowly add weight to her kart every 10 minute session and by the morning of the event's first day we were running lap times in the slowest 25 percent at race weight — this was awesome because she was no longer the slowest by a full second.

What neither of us expected was it would still be over 100 degrees during the day and at night things would only cool off to a chilly 80-90 degrees; this meant the inside of the facility was about 100 degrees all day! In addition to the heat, the loud noise and smell of exhaust gas at the indoor track meant both Jessica and I had intense headaches every day in Phoenix. The desire to compete, however, drove us both to push on.

Before the first competition of the event the race director explained to us pit stop and kart draw procedures. We were allowed to drop a kart if we did not like it and take the first undrawn one, which was very cool because I knew which karts Jessica drove well and which ones she did not. The downside to dropping a kart was forfeiting her qualifying position and starting at the rear of the field. That was a tough choice, but one I made for her in four out of five races.

For her first race, Jessica ran in the second heat and we drew a bad kart. We dropped that one and switched to a better kart, but that upset her some as she had to start 15th instead of 11th. When the green flag dropped, off she went and by the halfway point of the 30-minute heat Jessica was moving forward. I was talking to her on the radio, giving her lap times and spotting, while she was driving her heart out and passing other karts. With 10 minutes to go she was running eighth and working through slower traffic to make a run on seventh. With about five laps to go Jessica made the pass into seventh and that was where she finished, capturing the attention of everyone at the facility!

After the lunch break Jessica's teammates began to get more involved with supporting her as they could see she was there to compete. In her second heat race of the afternoon, Jessica moved up from eighth to finish fifth and that got the attention of other team managers and the race director. By that point we realized Jessica was going to have a respectable showing at the event, something that was very important to both of us. When we returned to the hotel room after the first day Jessica was sound asleep in 15 minutes! My little girl was wiped out!

I sat on the edge of my bed watching her sleep with pride and emotion welling up inside. Pam and I were so happy and glad we made the trip as a family. Pam now was also begging to take an interest in this racing stuff and became a very vocal advocate.

The track configuration for the second day was more technical, making it difficult to carry speed and placing a premium on the driver's skill. Even with this challenge and starting in the back due to kart swaps, Jessica managed to notch two more top-10 finishes. Jessica's second race of the day was the more interesting of the two because she was competing against the then top-ranked indoor female racer in the nation, Jean Hoye. Jessica was so excited about being in the race with Jean, but she was also disappointed because this woman treated Jessica with disrespect and mild contempt for no clear reason. Jessica was determined to earn the respect of this legendary racer, who was a veteran of many events such as the Indoor Nationals. Jessica had climbed in the overall points and was ahead of Jean going into the fourth heat of the day.

Jean started ahead of Jessica in the heat because, as usual by that point, we opted to swap karts and start in the back. Halfway through the race Jessica caught Jean and we began to take inventory of where she was strong and weak compared to the other drivers. Jessica and I discussed this numerous times on the radio and finally Jessica picked her passing point. She made a perfect run and was side-by-side, wheel-to-wheel with Jean and on the preferred line. Before I could get on the radio to warn her to be careful of a cheap shot, Jean turned into Jessica and drove her into the wall. Jessica made hard contact and lost three positions, but other than a few choice words over the radio with her spotter (Daddy), she was undaunted. Jessica gained back the three positions and found herself once again on Jean's back bumper.

Determined to make the pass, Jessica and I realized her best spot to get by was the same place on the track, but this time she would be wary of Jean not racing her clean. Jessica positioned herself for another pass and got side by side again when the unthinkable happened: Yup, Jean dumped Jessica into the wall for a second time in the exact same spot. Thirty people watching the race yelled their frustration and displeasure to the track officials, who did not see this dirty move for the second time.

Undaunted still, but with many very choice words over the radio and mild frustration, Jessica regained the positions again and was on Jean's bumper for a third time with just two laps to go. Jessica made her move and got almost side-by-side, once again with the preferred line, and you guessed it: Jean drove Jessica into the wall for the third time at the same place on the track.

Jessica, her Mom and Dad were all fit to be tied but several firm conversations with the race director did nothing to improve the finish. Jessica, Mom and Dad retired for the evening, anxious for the final race the next morning and no sooner did we get dinner finished at the hotel than Jessica was sleeping soundly and no doubt dreaming of a better way to pass Jean. Mom and I talked about the cheap shots for another hour before we also fell asleep.

For the third and final day of the event the track configuration was changed to a full-course layout and the duration of the race was an hour. As usual by then, we drew a kart we didn't like so we opted for an undrawn kart and a starting position of 20th. I told Jessica we needed her best drive and an earthquake could not have interrupted my determination to do all I could for her on the radio.

Fifteen minutes after the green flag dropped Jessica had gained five spots and 30 minutes into the hour-long race she was in 10th after methodically picking off one driver after another. With 15 minutes to go she was in seventh after making some breathtaking dive passes, but one bad pass with 10 laps to go cost her three spots and Jessica finished the race in 10th.

With just a few weeks of karting experience, Jessica placed 30th of the 60 drivers at the 2009 U.S. Indoor Nationals. You could not have found more proud parents.

CHAPTER 22 —ROTAX RACERS

Apex Karting of Tumwater, Washington, was clearly the best indoor facility in the state and it hosted competitions on Tuesday nights called the Apex Challenge Series (ACS). In her debut in the fall racing series, Jessica managed to place third overall in the light class, a pretty respectable showing. For the winter series there were three classes: Light (150 pounds), Medium (200 pounds) and Heavy (250 pounds). Jessica opted to compete in two classes each Tuesday night, Light and Medium. This was great fun for us because I spotted for her and helped on pit stop strategy, and she did what she does so well: drive.

One of her competitors in both classes during the winter series at Apex was Ben Wallace, who placed fourth at the Indoor Nationals in Phoenix. Ben was favored to win the Medium and Jessica was the favorite in the Light class. In qualifying for the first race of the series Jessica started second, behind Ben, in the Light class and fourth in the Medium. As the season progressed, Jessica and Ben were first and second in the standings and Ben was positioned to be the champion in both classes but for a breathtaking pass Jessica made on him in the second-to-last race of the series in the Medium class.

Jessica had followed Ben for nearly 10 laps in that race, knowing she could get by with a dive pass but to hold the position the move needed to be perfect. She looked inside after a long high-speed straightaway and Ben closed the door on her, putting Jessica back about three kart-lengths. Two more hard laps and Jess was again on Ben's bumper. He was protecting the inside so this time she looked outside, faking a pass to get him to move out on the next lap.

It worked perfectly and with two laps to go she drove hard inside when Ben expected an outside move, getting under and past en route to finishing ahead of him. That pass was cheered by both drivers and spectators that evening and as it turned out it also won Jessica the Medium class championship at the end of the season.

Jessica finished as the runner-up to Ben in the hunt for the Light championship and it was becoming clear we needed to explore the next step, the next level of kart competition for her.

During the winter months of 2010 Jessica set her sights on breaking the existing track records at Apex Karting and we also began racing on the .82-mile outdoor road course at PGP Motorsports Park in Kent, Washington. Jessica and I made several attempts at setting new benchmarks going both directions at Apex and in March 2010 with me on the radio as her spotter Jessica was able to set new track records for both the forward and reverse configurations at Apex.

Most teenagers enjoy sleeping in Saturday mornings, but Jessica and I would wipe the sleep out of our eyes at six in the morning, grab some extra clothes and take off in the pitch-black darkness and often cold wet winter mornings to race at PGP in the B-Spec winter series. These karts were a little faster than those at the indoor track and the course at PGP was massive compared to Apex. We learned early on that at outdoor venues we were not allowed to use radios, but I could give her hand signals during races and qualifying sessions. This presented some challenges as Jessica was very comfortable with the communication system we had established, but we quickly developed hand signals and learned early on we had the odd ability to know what the other was thinking at times.

It took Jessica three or four races at the new track to become proficient enough to compete for a podium finish in the B-Spec series and once she did, Jessica and I with some input from Mike Smith started discussing moving up to a Rotax kart. Speeds in a Rotax can top 80 mph, the horsepower was 30 or more and there was no protection around the tires; this was effectively an open-wheel machine. In addition to the much-increased speed and power, there were no seat belts and I needed some time to understand and become comfortable with that idea.

After talking to the local kart dealer and learning about many of the young kids who had been injured karting, I needed to discuss the pros and cons of a Rotax with Mom before a final decision could be made. After some effort was put into getting Mom comfortable with the idea of a faster kart, we decided to buy her an Arrow X9. The X9 we purchased was about three years old and it had an older motor that was down on power, but there we were: Rotax racers.

Our first big decision was picking a class to run in. Jessica was young and inexperienced enough to run in the Junior class, and everyone we talked to suggested that was the place for her to start. We were told the Senior class at PGP was very good and she would not be able to compete at that level for several years. I talked with Jessica about this and asked her what she wanted to do. She initially opted to run in the Junior class but I reminded her she would only get one year there before being too old. So, as usual for Jessica and Daddy, we decided as a team to go right into the Rotax Senior class and simply be happy if we did not get lapped.

I had no idea the motor we purchased was down on power, and frankly the first race I had no idea of what to do to improve the kart. I was afraid to touch anything and figured if it was not broke, don't fix it. Mike Smith helped out as part tuner, part coach and part counselor. Mike understood the chassis and basics of the motor but he was far from the level of the equipment experts that could be found walking around just about every pit. By contrast I was not even sure how to put gas in the kart!

At any rate, I was determined I would do things my way, not just like everyone else, and this became a tough lesson learned! This attitude came from my own experiences racing with my Dad and the success Jessica and I had drag racing ATVs in the sand. Wow, was I so wrong; there was nothing that carried over and it took me some time to realize it.

In early April we went to our first Rotax race at PGP and when pulling into the pits I noticed a large number of sponsored kart trailers and tuning experts working with special equipment. My, oh my. These guys took karting seriously!

On the track, Jessica was struggling with the physical demands of this new sport and was a little outside of her comfort level competing in the Senior class. Practice sessions showed we were three to four seconds off race pace and I had no idea how to fix that. I decided to take the approach that it would be more important to make the kart easier for her to drive even though I understood we would give up speed in doing so. As we approached qualifying Mike gave her a thumbs up and told her to go have fun and not to worry about where she qualified or finished. I leaned over and said "I love you, go have fun," and tapped the top of her helmet.

Jessica qualified 18th of 21 racers and there was some passing concern with her Mother and I that she may have reached her potential with indoor karting and this outdoor competition was just too much. I whispered to Pam, "Glad we only bought a used kart and motor!"

For the first heat race I tried to coach Jessica about getting a good start, going into the first turn and how careful to be, an issue I understood all too well, but she was too excited to hear a word I said. When the green flag dropped Jessica dove to the inside and tried to pass five karts at once — a big mistake. In the blink of an eye Jessica and her kart were three feet in the air, spinning slowly, and I held my breath because I was sure she would be hurt. But just like that she was back on the ground right-side-up and following the pack around the track. I think it took Mom and Dad a full minute to catch our breath and resume being spectators instead of concerned parents.

By two laps into her first Rotax race both Mom and I were cheering Jessica along as she made a pass for position, yelling hysterically like soccer parents every time their child touched the ball. I began to watch the race with a more critical eye now that we were on track facing other competitors, and it looked like we were down on power. I could also tell the kart was not handling worth beans and realized what a challenge it was going to be for her with me knowing nothing about the sport and not being a driver. At some point I was going to have to figure all of it out, both the kart and communicating with a 15-year-old girl about gearing, cornering and race tactics.

The heat race ended with Jessica in 15th, but she was smiling from ear to ear. I suspected the smile was to calm Mom and Dad down some as Jessica knew she was going to get an earful over the hard contact at the start of the race. Jessica, Mike and I sat in the pits talking as if we really knew what to do to make the kart faster and handle better for Jessica. Mike discussed corner entry and exit and I went over gearing and exit-off acceleration, but at the end of the day I have no idea what, if anything, we changed.

With the final about to start, I ran up to Jessica at the last second and with a cloud of two-stroke motor exhaust blowing in my face as karts were waved onto the track I yelled to her as loudly as I could over the noise to "be careful on the start this time," "have fun," and "I love you!"

After a warm-up lap the green flag waved and Jessica sped into the first turn again. This time I could see her back out a little and she made it cleanly around the corner and was off after the pack. At about the halfway point of the 15 laps I looked over at Mom and told her I thought Jessica was afraid, that she was driving fearful. The next lap I began waving my arms with a hint of encouragement and impatience at her to say *Okay, now let's get going!*

As if she heard me say "you know what to do, just do it," Jessica started to move forward, taking 12th and then 11th place while her lap times got faster and faster. A couple more laps and she was ninth and Mom and Dad were getting pretty excited because Jessica was gaining on the leaders. She took the white flag in eighth place and was closing on seventh with her kart chain broke, ending her race with a Did Not Finish (DNF).

My little girl walked up to me, perhaps feeling a little dejected and frustrated, with arms wide open and we hugged each other for several moments. I told her how proud I was and noted she was so fast after I waved at her to get going. She told me she hadn't seen me, but instead decided on her own that it was time to get going. We loaded up her broken kart and headed home after the trophy presentation.

I learned a lot from that first Rotax event: I could see we were under-powered, I could see I knew nothing about tuning or racing a Rotax kart, and I could see Jessica was a far more talented driver than she had pit crew or equipment. I could not drive for her, but I was determined to improve her crew and equipment, and my contribution to her pursuits.

CHAPTER 23 — SHE BEAT PASTRANA!!!!!!!!!!!!!!!!!!!!!!!!

April 22, 2010, was the kind of day we who have lived in this area would call a perfect spring day in the Pacific Northwest: sunny, not too hot and not too cold. The owner of PGP Motorsports Park had mentioned to Jessica and I at our last kart event that Travis Pastrana would be at the track for a charity rental kart race and exhibition on that day.

I said "Great, but who is Travis Pastrana?" and Jessica burst out with "Oh my God, Dad! You don't know who Travis Pastrana is?" I said "Sweetie, I don't" and she nearly yelled back with 15–year-old excitement: "*NITRO CIRCUS!*"

Oh! Then I remembered who he was. *Nitro Circus* was a TV show on MTV which showcased Travis Pastrana as perhaps the world's greatest extreme motorsports star. A multiple X-Games gold-medal winner, Pastrana had a full motocross course and a waterslide carved into a hillside at home. Base jumping, sky diving, riding and driving — he did it all and I was thrilled that Jessica would get the chance to meet this amazing talent, who I was just finding out was something of an idol to her.

I pulled Jessica out of school at noon and we drove the hour to the track, which was packed with people a full two hours before the event was to begin. Mom and I had discussed the event and whether or not she should take off work to go with us. I really had no idea what to expect and let Pam decide what she wanted to do. She opted to stay at work and let us keep her updated with phone calls and email because I had no idea of what would happen at the event.

Jessica brought her helmet just in case there was a chance to race with Pastrana, Dave Mira and the six other professional rally car drivers who would be there, but it was not until we got to the track that we found out the procedures in place. Even though she would have been a popular choice with the 4,000 people there, Jessica would not be automatically selected to race. Instead, she would have to take part in the charity raffle and have her name drawn. I quickly assessed our options as I was not going to be able to talk her into the race or even buy a seat.

I had about $200 in my wallet, but figured I would need to keep $50 for emergencies, leaving $150 for raffle tickets. I would pay at least $150 to get her into the race outright, so buying the same amount in tickets was an easy decision. Being Jessica's chief strategist, I had her buy 50 tickets just as they opened sales, 50 more at the halfway point and finally 50 just as they were closing sales. I figured it would be better to spread out our chances as we were just one of 400 people buying tickets for the chance to race with Pastrana.

An announcer grabbed a microphone and started telling the crowd about the event and how the drawing would work and the race run. He added some tickets drawn would be for prizes like shirts and hats instead of the chance to race. Sure enough, just as Jessica and I were saying to each other that we hoped we didn't end up with a hat — you guessed it — one of her tickets was draw for a hat.

She walked up to get her prize hat, and we were both slightly disappointed. But, we still had a handful of tickets so we tried to look ahead and our excitement level stayed high. A few more tickets were drawn for prizes, making some kids pretty happy, and then they started to draw for the 12 people who would race with Pastrana.

The first ticket wasn't us, or the second or third or fourth. By the time the tenth ticket was drawn we were feeling pretty unlucky. But then the eleventh and twelfth tickets were pulled and — *BINGO!* — one of the final two seats in the race belonged to us. We were so excited Jessica and I jumped three feet off the ground hugged each other so hard everyone around us probably thought we had just won the lottery.

Two more tickets ended up being drawn for a reason that escapes me and one of those also belonged to Jessica, so she promptly gave it to her friend Tony who came to the event hoping to race Pastrana as well.

Jessica took off at a run to the car to get her helmet, with its signature flame paint job, and racing shoes, covering the 900 yards there and back in what seemed like 15 seconds. Out of breath from rushing, I held her phone, shoes and sunglasses so she could get dressed. After that I went to check out the rental karts lined up for the event.

I wanted to get her into kart 12 because it was her lucky number and her race number, and in past races we knew it was one of the stronger karts in PGP's fleet. I figured being the "chief strategist" that this was my small contribution to give her a shot at competing with these professional racers. I found kart 12 and placed her gloves in the seat to reserve it because the other drivers were also looking over the available karts and making their selections. But, while I was off looking for my driver, who had taken a health break, another driver took Jessica's gloves off the seat of kart 12 and moved them to the seat of the kart in front of it. By the time we got back to the line of karts this other guy was sitting in kart 12 and all of the strongest karts had been taken.

I picked the strongest middle-of-the-pack kart from the ones that were left, but Jessica was not impressed with my choice, kart 14. I told her it was just for qualifying and we could try to get a better kart during the draw for the pre-final and final. I reminded her kart 14 turned very well to the right and the motor was strong, so given the direction of the track configuration she would be okay. To be fair to the track, all the rental karts were very evenly matched, so close that it would take an exceptional driver to notice the difference in cornering. That same exceptional driver would also know how to adapt and adjust lines and driving style to compensate for any differences. As for top speed, the karts were effectively dead even.

The race director set the grid and Jessica would start 16th of the 20 racers for the six-lap qualifying session. Travis Pastrana started on the pole with Dave Mira second and the balance of the pro rally drivers filling out the remaining spots in the top eight for the single-file start. After a warm-up lap the grid was set and the green flag dropped. Jessica passed four karts on the straightaway headed into the first turn but the professionals began to pull away from the pack just a half a lap into the race.

By the second lap Jessica was running just behind the rally drivers and she began to methodically pick them off one after another. With one lap to go she passed Mira and on the last corner of the last lap Jessica drove around

Pastrana, who had been unchallenged up to that point. Jessica won the qualifying round and would start on the pole! The crowd of several thousand went crazy when Jessica passed Pastrana, shocking me a little, but I was smiling from ear to ear. I had just watched my little girl make the best drive I had ever seen, getting every ounce from the kart that it had to give.

When Jessica and Pastrana drove into the pits I could see her eyes were focused on me, but she was required to stay seated until all karts had been shut off. Pastrana yelled something to Jessica over the noise of the still-running karts, but to this day I don't know what he said. Whatever it was, I could tell Jessica liked it; she was beaming. He bent over backwards to make sure Jessica knew how impressed he was with her drive. When the drivers were free to get out of the karts they all started talking about the race, so I waited patiently for Jessica to come over to me. After what seemed like an hour she ran up to me and we hugged liked we hadn't seen each other in 10 years. I had to fight back tears and managed to say "I love you" only about 200 times.

Perhaps a hundred people approached me to tell me how amazed they were with Jessica's drive and to ask how many years she had been racing. It was interesting to see shock on their faces when I told them that was her first year. I called Mom at work and told her what had just happened and she was so excited but also sad about not seeing it in person. I told her I would email from my phone and call every moment I could.

When it was time for the pre-final the race director announced Jessica would start on the pole, Pastrana second and so on down the line until all 20 drivers were named. He also selected the row from which karts would be assigned, pointing to the row on the right and — dumb luck! — sure enough kart 12 was there in the first position. Jessica and I smiled at each other and we each knew she would have a good drive. The green flag dropped and Jessica started to drive away from Pastrana and the other drivers, and by the midway point she had a half-lap lead. Jessica never looked back and by the time she took the checkered flag she was another zip code away from Pastrana and the rest of the field, with Mira finishing fourth.

Jessica jumped out of kart 12 and flew into my arms; yup, we did it again: hugging and laughing. We were simply having the time of our lives and were determined to win the whole thing! When Pastrana got out of his kart he went right to Jessica and said how impressed he was with her drive, and they talked about it like lifelong racers.

Just when we thought the final was in the bag because kart 12 was again in the first position where Jessica would start, Dave Mira went to the race director and told him bluntly that she would not drive kart 12 again. Instead, he decided he would drive kart 12 for the final and Jessica would drive the kart he just gotten out of, kart 2. I don't know if he thought there was a practical joke being played or if it was a setup of some sort, but he was not all that pleasant about his demand to drive kart 12 for the final. The race director approached me, shrugged and said he was sorry, but what could he do? I told him it would be no problem, that we'd be fine.

Jessica looked at me as if she expected me to fix it so she would get kart 12 back; she clearly was not sure what to think of what had just happened. Kart 2 was a decent kart but it did not turn to the right very well, which was the direction she would be going in the final. I put my arm around Jessica and told her we would be okay, and I asked her to move her line out about four feet so she would carry more corner speed. I also reminded her even though she would start fourth and not on the pole, the better drivers with the better karts still had to get past her, so as long as she got everything the kart had to give she would be fine.

After the warm-up lap the field came around the last turn to take the green flag with a rolling start. Starting fourth after the kart switch, Jessica was on the outside lane entering turn 1 and had hard contact with the fifth-place kart bumping her back a spot going into the sharp right-hander. Following my directions about taking a wider line and keeping speed up, Jessica came out of the turn passing both the fifth- and third-place racers. Sitting in third, she figured out how to get the less-than-desired kart moving and by the end of the first lap she was closing on Mira and Pastrana, who were first and second respectively.

Jessica got around Pastrana by passing him in a fast sweeper about halfway through the final and then she passed Mira for the lead with about four laps to go. Not able to gap Mira or Pastrana by much more than a few kart lengths, Jessica was getting all she could out of kart 2. Tony Severson, a U.S. Army solider and ranked kart driver also known as "Exit Wound," also made his way past Pastrana and Mira to challenge Jessica from second place. Jessica ended up winning the event by eight inches over the hard-charging Severson and the 4,000 people watching went crazy.

In the pits Mira jumped out of kart 12 as if he was upset about something and approached Jessica, but his expression was friendly and open and he proceeded to tell her what a great drive she had and how impressed he was with her driving. Pastrana hopped out of his kart and gave Jessica a high-five and they celebrated the end of the race with his buddies and the fans. While I can't say this for sure, I think nearly all of the 20 racers congratulated Jessica.

While she was sharing this experience with her fellow drivers and talking about the race with everyone including fans, I patiently waited so she could enjoy the moment. Then something clicked and she turned away from everyone and ran to me and we hugged again, but this time it was a little shorter because she knew her fellow racers might be watching.

I let Jessica hang out with the racers while I called Mom to update her. I had emailed a couple of times to say she was leading, she was winning, and she's out front; but I had to call to tell her "SHE BEAT PASTRANA!" I could sense from Mom's tone she was crushed not to be able to see this event or experience this for herself. I was also sad for Pam and promised myself that Jessica's Mom would be more involved from then on.

There was something special taking shape and Mom needed to be part of it.

CHAPTER 24 — JEFF GORDON

Shortly after the Pastrana event, Mike Smith informed me he had made arrangements for Jessica to race a kart in Charlotte, North Carolina, against four-time NASCAR Cup Series champion Jeff Gordon and some other great drivers at Gordon's foundation fundraiser event. Mike participated in the fundraiser the previous year and he thought Jessica could possibly be competitive with Gordon at his event. Mom, Dad and Jessica — maybe even Charlie the dog — were tremendously excited and terrified all at the same time about this opportunity.

As we got closer to our departure date, Mike, who was going to travel with us, confided in me that he was a little concerned Jessica may not find the pace in just a day or two to be competitive at a track that was new, especially going up against a professional racer as good as Jeff Gordon. Jessica's appearance was sponsored by Pacific Technical Resources, owned two of the nicest guys in the world. Mike wanted to make sure I knew Bud and Jay wanted to win the event, not just bring a little girl down to race. I told Mike if Jessica was serious about racing, she needed to take advantage of this amazing opportunity.

Mom, doing her usual Mom stuff, made sure we were packed with everything and anything we could need or want. She did it so efficiently we checked just three bags for an eight-day trip 2,000 miles from home. We flew all night and arrived in Charlotte around six or seven in the morning. The three of us were so tired we wanted to head straight to the hotel to get a couple hours sleep, but Mike said he wanted to be at the track when it opened; Jessica needed laps and plenty of them if she was going to be able to run at pace with one of the best drivers in the world.

Forget sleep, off to the track we went. I am not sure who grumbled the loudest, Jessica, me or Mom.

For the first two or three hours of practice Jessica was still feeling the effects of the all-night plane trip. None of us was in a terribly upbeat mood, but we were determined to get the track down so she kept at it. While we were taking a short break, I noticed a whiteboard with the names of several of the best drivers in NASCAR and their lap times. I don't recall too many of those names now, but I recall looking at Jessica's times and comparing them to the NASCAR guys, and feeling some trepidation.

We were more than two seconds slower than those guys and I wasn't sure Jessica had the ability to gain that much speed in just a day or two. But, one practice session after another, Jessica kept getting better and better, and just as she had done in Phoenix at the Indoor Nationals, once we learned which kart she was fastest in I tried to make sure she got back into it multiple times to get her confidence up. It worked, and by the end of practice the first day she was only one second off the pace.

The next morning the King's Cup event was scheduled, another charity race hosted by seven-time NASCAR champion Richard "The King" Petty that was to raise money for paralyzed veterans. Several NASCAR drivers, including those from Petty's team at the time, were scheduled to take part.

By mid-morning Jessica had lowered her lap times to within one-tenth of a second of the track record, which got the attention of everyone there and led to an invite for her to race on Team Media for the King's Cup. Her teammates included NASCAR Cup driver Joey Logano, reporters from the ESPN and SPEED-TV networks, and other media people including Riki Rachtman, host of the *Racing Rocks!* weekly radio show and frequent contributor to SPEED-TV and NASCAR.com.

Surrounded by all these racing insiders, our 15-year-old little girl was having the time of her life and she was determined to make the most of the opportunity. There were so many amazing drivers at the event I don't recall all the names but NASCAR stars Paul Menard, AJ Allmendinger, Kurt Busch, and brothers Elliot and Hermie Sadler come to mind, to name a few.

As the teams began to form, I got a few photos and Joey Logano pulled Team Media in close to discuss race strategy: Logano wanted to win the King's Cup! Meanwhile, Riki and the other reporters were there to have fun and I was just having a blast being part of it. After giving Jessica a look of amusement, Joey suggested he pull the 30-minute stint, his buddy Brandon take a 15-minute stint and Jessica and the reporters fulfill the mandatory five minute-per-driver stints in the middle.

All the guys on the team decided Jessica should represent Team Media at the draw for starting positions, but wouldn't you know it: out of the 16 teams in the event she drew number 16. You could tell Joey and Brandon were each a little disappointed the blonde lucky charm started the team dead last.

Knowing Jessica was terrific in traffic I encouraged Joey to let her run the first 10 minutes; being a competitor he said okay but if she struggled he would pull her out. I agreed, and as Jessica and I were talking on the radio before warm-up laps to start, she asked me "Do you think my team hates me for getting 16th starting position?" I told her I didn't think so, but they would sure like you a lot more if you could find a way to move forward and gain some positions during your stint. The race was only an hour so we needed to make up as much track position as possible, as quickly as possible.

The green flag was dropped and off Jessica went, starting 16th racing against many of NASCAR's elite drivers. Five minutes into her run she gained six spots and was running 10th, with Jessica and I on the radio planning every pass and having a ball. By the end of the second five minutes she was up to fourth and Joey wanted to get in the kart. I got on the radio and said "You did it, kiddo, you gave your team a chance. Let's pit next lap." I waited until the pit was clear and Joey was ready, and they did the driver exchange. Joey got out on the track and his skills were immediately obvious, he was laying down laps about two-tenths faster than Jessica and he kept moving forward, regaining the spots lost during the pit stop. As I recall he got as high as third place before contact on track and a bad pit stop for another driver change put us back to sixth.

We did not win anything in the King's Cup, but pats on the back from everyone on her team and that was worth it for Jessica and Daddy! Joey asked me at one point in the event what she raced and I told him nothing, we just started karting a few months ago — he looked at me with a puzzled look on his face for a moment and then went about his business.

The next day was the Gordon event and we arrived at the track as soon as they opened the doors. We would only have a couple hours for practice before they closed the track for the charity race. After a handful of practice runs that morning we went back to the hotel to rest and prepare for the event.

Later that day as we left the hotel to head back to the track, Mike Smith gave us the lowdown on how the race would be conducted. All participants would change karts every practice and every qualifying run, except Jeff Gordon who stayed in kart 24 (his NASCAR number). Mike added Jeff would get faster and faster as the day went on. The top 12 drivers in qualifying got into the race, Mike said, while the other 80 or so would be watching. No pressure at all!

Jessica's team was selected for a private practice session with the event host before the qualifying rounds started and I got to watch my little girl drive the course with NASCAR champion Jeff Gordon, veteran NASCAR racer Kenny Wallace, 2010 national karting champion John Kimbral, 2009 national karting champion Mike Smith and many other notable and amazing talents including Bud and Jay, who were pretty fair drivers in their own right.

If you don't know it, Jeff Gordon is a very trim, well-conditioned athlete and not all that tall, which is an advantage in a kart. He was also a kind, gracious and generous person out of the kart — but once he strapped in, he was a racer.

I was on the radio with Jessica as she was gaining on Jeff in practice, and she asked me if she should pass him. I told her "Sure, but whatever you do please, please try to make it clean." Jessica's lap times were right there with Jeff, who was relearning the track and seeing how his kart was handling. Even with that, there were only a couple drivers who were as fast as Jeff during that practice session. Jessica got on the radio again and said "Daddy, I can pass him, should I do it?" I told her to go for it! I watched every move Jessica made and then she did it: she got a run on Jeff and drove around him, never touching him.

Just as Mike said, Jeff got faster and faster and faster but Jessica was able to pass him again during the second practice session. At the end of that practice Jeff climbed out of his kart and went right to Jessica to talk about racing. He acknowledged her clean passes, making her one happy little girl and Mom and Dad proud and happy parents.

When qualifying started each driver on the team would get about three chances to lay down his or her best lap. Going out early was usually not good as the track would be greener; Jessica would make her qualifying runs in races five, seven and eight, meaning she would go out on a better track but also that she had less room to make a mistake or get a bad kart draw.

Watching the big scoreboard, Jeff was usually the fastest driver, and — again as Mike Smith predicted — he was getting faster and faster each run. When Jessica was called up to make her first run she drew kart 16, which was a strong kart. Qualifying is all about turning a fast lap so experienced drivers try not to race each other while the inexperienced bang away on each other and jockey for position.

I used the radio to keep Jessica in clean air as best I could and when I looked up at the scoreboard she was on top for her race and had the fastest lap of the day! John Kimbral, the 2010 national champion was a mere tenth of a second behind Jess for the pole position and Jeff Gordon was the third fastest. So John went out again with Jeff and each of them topped the chart with new fast laps. Jessica was in the final race but after their runs she would be starting third on the grid as it stood then.

Jessica went out for her second run and she put down a blisteringly fast lap, putting her once again on the top of the chart and in line for pole position unless someone else got lucky or Jeff found speed he had not yet shown. I recall looking up at the scoreboard and thinking back to Jessica's first kart event in sleepy Tumwater when she topped the board and set fast lap. To say the least, emotions were running wild for Mom and I. It was so hard to believe our/my little girl was doing this right in front of us when just mere months ago we were talking about fishing trips to Alaska and buying a horse.

Jessica gave her final qualifying run to her teammate Shannon Macintosh, giving Shannon one last attempt at qualifying. Shannon, who is frankly just a stunningly attractive and talented young lady, is also an amazing driver. At that time she was racing oval tracks near Indianapolis and was just barely off the pace to get the final starting position for the event. I helped the

120

track guys with Shannon's kart draw and coached her as best I could, and with some tips from Mike Smith and others Shannon went out and got the 13th and final starting position using Jessica's final qualifying spot.

The next big challenge we faced was the final, which was 10 minutes long. The original plan was for the starting field to be fully inverted, meaning Jeff Gordon would start dead last with Jessica in front of him and John Kimbral in front of her. As if that wasn't going to be hard enough, Jessica drew an average kart, not one of the two I wanted. I am not exactly sure what happened, but at this point some discussion occurred with the track owner and Jeff, and then he announced the grid would be set by qualifying — no invert! I am not exactly sure who made this decision, but I suspect it had something to do with the quality of the drivers and how challenging it would be for Jeff and Jessica to come through the field in just 10 minutes. Also, by this time Jeff was getting tired as he had been driving almost non-stop for nearly an hour and a half.

We were in Charlotte, NASCAR's capital and Jessica was starting from the pole she earned with four-time NASCAR champion Jeff Gordon starting second – how does a father begin to explain the feeling at that moment? Yes, these were just karts but those were some of the best drivers in the world out there competing against my little girl!

The race would begin with a standing start and staggered grid, meaning Jessica on pole was slightly ahead of Jeff. I told her to be careful when the green flag dropped; she would have a small gap but with cold tires she needed to drive smart and not start to push until her tires warmed up after three or four laps. Jessica replied "Daddy, this kart sucks!" I calmed her down and told her I watched the kart before and I knew it did not turn well to the left, but it was still strong.

After the start Jeff showed right away why he was one of the best drivers in the world. On cold tires he closed in on Jessica very quickly and after one lap he was on her bumper looking for a spot to pass. John Kimbral was also pushing to the front fast, and I told Jessica calmly by that point she should have enough heat in the tires to start pushing a little harder because Jeff and John were on her tail.

Jessica was under enormous pressure and I could see she was just a little off on corner speed and braking, so I told her she needed to relax and focus on the places where we were getting beat by Jeff and John. Although she cleaned it up the kart was just a little off so we still were slower, but thankfully for us John and Jeff started racing each other. At that point her tires were now warm so Jessica began to pull away and gain a small gap of four or five kart-lengths.

At the midpoint of the race, just as I was beginning to get comfortable with her pace and lead, Jessica got on the radio and told me "Daddy, the kart is going away, I am losing grip." I told her to move her line out just a little so she could carry more speed, but as soon as she did John passed Jeff and quickly ran up on Jessica. Here is where the radios helped. I told her: "Jessica, John is coming, he is looking on the inside," so she changed her line from one lap to the next to confuse him as to where she would be on corner entry. I reminded her to make him drive the longer track: if he was going to pass make him do it on the outside.

John was clearly faster the final three laps but I give him all the credit in the world. He had three chances to pass Jessica, but each would have resulted in pretty hard contact to move her out of position. Instead, John decided if he was going to pass her it was going to be clean and for that I was so very thankful. With the white flag in the air, Jessica asked me with some tension in her voice if John was going to pass her but I said "Not if you drive perfect!" Her last lap was perfect and the scoreboard showed Jessica Dana in first place, John Kimbral second and Jeff Gordon third.

Once all the karts had completed the cool down lap after the checkered flag and were parked on the track, Jessica and Jeff spent a few minutes talking about the race. John joined them and then the entire field of drivers joined in. Jeff was so gracious and kind, allowing me to take many pictures — he was just a class act. Bud and Jay, too, were just the greatest guys and we will forever be thankful for the opportunity.

Jessica did a couple post-race interviews and out of nowhere John Bickford, Jeff Gordon's stepfather, stopped by our table to tell us how much he enjoyed watching Jessica race. He mentioned she was very talented and that it caught Jeff by surprise to see that little girl pass him. We enjoyed our conversation with John and I am so grateful for the counsel he gave me.

The event ended with a dinner and Jeff presented Jessica with a trophy for winning the event. My wife and I sat at a different table so Jessica and the other racers from her team could eat with Jeff at his table. Neither Pam nor I said anything at the time, but I think each of us has the same thought: things were going to change.

CHAPTER 25 — SHE OWNS FIVE TRACK RECORDS AT 15

We returned from Charlotte to a hero's welcome in Tumwater. Jessica appeared on SPEED-TV and hundreds of people followed us daily while we were in Charlotte. Now with the confidence and knowledge that Jessica had the skill to drive with the best in the world, we again turned our focus to Rotax karts.

At the same time we were talking about getting Jessica into a full-sized, 650-horsepower race car and I began looking for a Super Stock late-model race car and a suitable crew chief. We wanted to know if there was another big step to take in front of us; the plan was to get her into the car before the end of the summer to see how she responded to the weight and speed.

In my search for a crew chief and a possible alignment with a local team, I had numerous conversations about moving Jessica up to a Late Model despite her having no time at all in any type of race car. Those familiar with racing warned me Jessica could not make the jump: it was too fast, too dangerous, she had no experience and she would get eaten alive by drivers who had hundreds and hundreds of thousands of laps at the speedway.

Another concern was money.

Up until this point we had been able to keep pace with karting racing expenses, but we realized this next phase with a Late Model would be very expensive. More to the point, my lack of knowledge about the sport was going to become more expense then we would ever imagine. One of John Beckford's parting statements to me was be careful and to keep my "pen in my pocket," away from my checkbook.

On two previous karting events I hired "tuners" to help us at the track. Both were well-known in the Pacific Northwest and one was known internationally, so I figured we couldn't lose. The first I paid just $300, but the real cost was to my confidence. I was told that everything I said and did was wrong, and everything I wanted to do was wrong. I let this man take the lead for an event and while he did manage to keep us running until the end of the race, Jessica and I looked at each after the event and agreed we wouldn't use him again.

The second guy was Tim Musch, who is just simply brilliant when it comes to karts. After talking to Tim, I paid him to coach Jessica and I for our third Rotax race. Tim pointed out issues with the kart, he helped Jessica address some little things with her line and braking, and he helped me better understand that I knew nothing about set-up and race strategy — but he was kind about it. Tim was generous with his knowledge and time, and he was a great help to us. He also reminded me to keep our expectations low, that level of karting was very competitive and Jessica had a lot to learn. He also noted I too had a lot to learn and until Jessica and I got on the same page to just enjoy the racing, gain experience and don't worry about top-five finishes for a year or more.

It was at this same race we brought Matt Kindrick on board to help out in the pits. Matt is a nearly 6-foot former rugby player with a short brown hair and shoulders wider then a VW Bug. His kind soul and gentle demeanor masks a fierce competitive fire in his belly. We met Matt at a Jiffy Lube and told him we needed someone to help with the karts and possibly a race car. He said "I am in, tell me where to be and when!" We liked Matt instantly: a guy who barely knew how to change oil in a passenger car was now going to crew for a 15-year-old high school sophomore racing high-performance karts, ATVs and race cars in the near future.

In August 2010 we took Matt along to a two-day Rotax race at PGP Motorsports Park. The event was held over the weekend, Saturday and Sunday, and we were still looking to score our first podium finish in Rotax karts; Jessica's best finish to that point was fifth. My confidence was not all the great about setting up the kart but I did notice Jessica was getting better and better despite different tuners, track conditions and challenges with the kart.

Going into the event, Matt, Jessica and I had learned a lot from Tim and from talking to others. We also learned that Jessica's inexperience compared to other racers when it came to giving feedback about the kart meant we needed to watch her closely on track so that we could understand what she was trying to tell us. Of course, Matt and I were inexperienced too, so we talked a lot and made the set-up changes that we thought might help to compensate for what we didn't know. At that event we really learned how much we didn't know.

Saturday morning was a perfect Northwest day for any outdoor activity, racing being no exception. Matt and I were determined to figure out how to do a better job in the pits for Jessica and we would not have the assistance of a "tuner" as I decided it was time to figure this out on our own. We started working at six in the morning, squaring the front, changing tires — by the way, Matt changed kart tires with his bare hands, we were sure lucky he was such a nice guy! — and by nine we were prepared for the first practice of the day.

We sent Jessica out with what we thought was a good set-up, but after a few laps she brought the kart in; we forget to loosen the steering stem! She went back out, laid down a couple of fast laps and gave us a thumbs up: she liked the kart. This was a good start to the day for our inexperienced team, and we all felt better about the upcoming races. As the day went on we got faster and faster, so much so that Jessica started the final race from third place on the grid.

Fourteen laps into the final, Jessica was holding on to third and Matt, Pam and I were on edge, hoping we would be able to get that first Rotax podium. With the tension and nervousness we felt, the last lap took what seem like an hour to complete but to our complete joy Jessica finished third; we had our first podium finish in our fourth race. There was not a more proud team walking around the pits than us after that. You would have thought we won the entire darn race, but we didn't care. We had our first trophy and we were going to celebrate until the next morning when we had another race to prepare for.

That night I felt content but I just could not sleep. I ran the race in my head and thought about the kart set-up over and over again, and by five Sunday morning I was outside in the dark with a flashlight and work lights from the back of the trailer working on the kart. I was positive I had an idea to find speed: move the center of gravity back on the kart. I would lower the spindles, shift the weight, change air pressure, change gearing to increase top speed, and change toe-in — but without the fancy lasers other teams had. I was going to make this adjustment using unconventional tools: eyesight and a straight edge! It was ultra-aggressive but for some reason based on what we did the day before I was convinced we could be faster.

As Matt and I prepared Jessica for her first practice session on Sunday, I told her the kart might be fast, or I might have completely screwed it up. If it was fast, I wanted her to change her line and drive randomly so the other drivers would not know how fast we were or what our line was. If it was a dog, I wanted her to come in right away so we could undo everything I did. Jessica came in from the practice all smiles; she came over and said "Oh my gosh, was I fast Dad." We were all smiles but I was convinced I could find more speed so before the second practice session I made two more minor changes.

For the second practice I told Jessica she might be even faster and if so don't let anyone know what we have and get off the track if the kart was good. Six to eight laps of practice and Jessica came off the track just beaming: "Dad, the kart is so fast." Now we had to see how we would fare at qualifying.

Matt threw on new sticker tires and we calculated the fuel load to have us come off the track one pound over the minimum 365. We made sure Jessica left the pits first to make her qualifying run and three laps into it she was five-tenths of a second faster than everyone. Six laps in and she was still four-tenths better than second place so I had her come off the track and run over the scales to make sure we made weight. She passed over the scales and we were fine; meaning we had just won the pole position for the first time in a Rotax kart, her fifth race ever!

This was a major accomplishment for us and we were so darn excited we looked like a bunch of high school kids being silly. Jessica was still lacking experience compared to all the other racers, but she was starting from the pole and she was driving like she was just as good as anyone on the track!

I knew the start for the pre-final race would be an issue and sure enough, it was. Coming out of the first turn after the green flag, Jessica was in second place, partly from the gear change and partly from some contact that caused her to lose a great deal of track position. Just then first place began to drive away and we thought Jessica would end up finishing second or maybe even worse — meaning we would be starting second on the grid for the final — if she could not get that spot back.

And then out of nowhere Jessica started closing the gap and three laps into the pre-final she was on the bumper of first place. Determined to keep Jessica behind him, the first-place driver kept looking over his shoulder every 15 seconds so he would know when she was coming and where she was coming from. That strategy was sound, but it backfired when he over-drove a corner and left the track, moving Jessica into first place.

Pam, Matt and I cheered loud enough that everyone in the pits heard us; not for the other driver leaving the track but for our kid taking the lead. We were learning how to win at that very moment, as a driver Jessica was learning and as a crew we were learning. After Jessica took the checkered flag for the pre-final she drove over the scales and we made weight, meaning we were finally on pole for the final.

To get ready for the final Matt and I checked every nut and bolt, and second-guessed every set-up decision we had made. We wanted to make changes to find more speed, and after much agonizing over "do we or don't we make a change," we decided on a minor chassis change. Jessica bellowed "DON'T CHANGE IT!" but we did anyway.

When Jessica lined up on pole for the final we were so anxious that Pam, Matt and I all felt like we were going to throw up. We were fairly sure it was not our lunch but nerves. On the other hand, Jessica was as cool as a cucumber and it showed: in the pits she was loose, happy and ready to race.

Her class was lined up and sent out on the track, the green flag dropped and Jessica took off! She got a fairly good start but because of the gearing change she was slightly slower off the start; still, she looked great and for a moment the kart looked perfect. Matt and I were just about to start celebrating when Jessica slowed-up entering into the first turn and was hit from behind by a rival competitor. The impact was very hard, bending her back-bar six inches forward, which meant the chassis suddenly got very tight — the front wouldn't turn when steering was applied — and it also created a side bite condition making the kart jerk hard at the apex of the corners.

Jessica had no choice now but to drive her heart out; it was all her, the set-up was gone. She didn't have the ability to drive a relaxed race with a fast kart, now she had a fast kart but it was a monster to drive. On top of that every corner was hurting her ribs, but she still had blazing top-end speed thanks to the very tall gear we were pulling.

At the midway point of the final she developed a sizeable lead before her tires got too warm and the ill-handling kart began to tire her out physically. She started to slow down, we could see it, and Mom, Matt and I were nearly in a panic. All three of us were thinking something was wrong, the kart was going away, something was broke — you name it, we thought it. She had the lead, the race was hers to win, but she was losing a second per lap and second place was coming on like a freight train.

When the white flag was waved she needed to hang on for just one more lap, but we could tell she was physically exhausted. Luck was on our side, however, and Jessica held on to take first place. Pandemonium was the best word to describe the celebration in our pit.

A few moments later we learned that Jessica had set a new track record for that class in that direction. After the celebration and backslapping, I told Jessica how nervous I had been about her getting passed because she was losing time. She said "Daddy, you dork! I slowed down to save my kart and rest; I was tired but I watched second place and just made sure he did not get too close." All I could do was smile and think to myself: *she just thinks we're racing*! After passing tech at the end of the race Jessica was pronounced the winner! We did it!

At that point Jessica owned two track records at Apex Karting in Tumwater, Washington, for going both directions on the old configuration, and at the time of this writing she holds three track records at PGP: TaG Senior, both directions, and Rotax Senior in the clockwise direction.

CHAPTER 26 — WE BOUGHT A BANANA? MORE LIKE A LEMON

When Pam and I decided to go ahead and purchase Jessica a race car after many family conversations, the first challenge was financial. We just didn't have any extra money; our real estate business was gone, mostly from the company that had purchased it but also after being negatively impacted by the economy. My personal book of business had been nearly destroyed due to some very bad legal advice. Given that, how do we find the money to buy a race car and equipment? Equally daunting was what type of race car and what equipment would we need? As previously noted ATVs and auto racing are absolutely disparate sports and very little of my racing or knowledge carried over, much to my utter disappointment.

I talked to dozens of sellers all over the country, each telling me why their car was the best one available for the money, how many championships the car had won, etc. Some even listed the names of big-time race car drivers who had once driven their car. I was overwhelmed; intuitively I knew most of these guys were nothing more then used-car or snake-oil salesman and after talking to me for a minute they could tell I was a sucker, I was fresh meat and I would believe about anything.

Rather than trying to bluff them into thinking I knew what I was talking about, I took the approach of sharing with them my story about Jessica, hoping to connect with someone so that I could take comfort in doing a deal. Each and every guy I talked to who was interested in our story told me to watch out for everyone else, saying in racing everyone tries to take advantage of you and you will learn through your wallet — but I could trust them for some reason. It was not that I did not believe this, but I felt strongly if I could talk to the right guy, someone with a conscience, then we would be okay.

To solve our money problem our strategy was to trade my hot rod, a 1966 Shelby Cobra that I invested about $60,000 in when I built it myself in 2004. The Cobra was black and nasty fast with a small-block 427 that delivered 500 hp. The Cobra was the car of my dreams when I was in my 20s, and Pam and I enjoyed many date nights in the summer in it. I didn't learn until after it was gone that Pam had enjoyed that car and our date nights nearly as much as I had. Even today, I feel terrible about losing that car as it meant a great deal to her and I both.

I put out an Internet ad offering my Cobra in trade and emails came in from every corner of the nation. I had tons of opportunities but after dozens and dozens of conversations I talked to a car owner in California and we seemed to make a positive connection. We exchanged photos of the cars and I told him our story. In reply he told me his car had been used by his daughter who had raced karts and then stock cars on road courses. As a successful businessman, he would make me a great deal. He convinced me his yellow road course car had a Bristol Champion Chassis — referring to the famed NASCAR oval track in Tennessee that was similar to the track in Washington we would be racing at — and he had all the necessary oval-track parts for it. It was an amazing car, he said, but to make the deal even better for me he would throw in all kinds of extra parts.

For some reason, I just could not get comfortable with the seller or his proposed deal. When I think he sensed I was no longer interested in his car, he called and said: "Tell you what I will do; I will throw in a $35,000 TOE motor, it has only six races on it and you could drive it for another season, just change the oil." He told me the TOE was a 670 hp motor and the motor installed in the car was absolutely fresh and would make 700 hp. How could I go wrong? Between the two motors alone, he said "I am paying for your car with $70,000 in motors."

Convinced that we were now being offered a great deal, Jessica, her friend Natasha and I decided to take a road trip to California to trade my street-legal race car for one that did circles on an oval track. We made a fun trip out of the long, boring drive to central California, but when we arrived at the seller's place I was already getting impatient about the return trip.

The seller had an amazing shop with tons of equipment, cars and motors, and when we walked through the doors I started feeling a little more at ease with our deal. I thought: *We're going to be okay, he won't rip me off, right*? We each looked closely at our respective trades, I started the Cobra and the 500 hp motor came to life in the blink of an eye as always. The car was spotless, the trailer was spotless and with two extra sets of wheels and tires and lots of extra parts, he quickly realized he was getting a pretty great deal.

When we walked up to the yellow "banana" it was not the same as we saw in the pictures for sure. It was dirty and actually looked like a pile of crap, but the owner was quick to tell me how fast it was and how amazing the car was. Not paying close attention, I didn't realize the shocks were different, the transmission was changed and the valve covers were different. I could not get over the fact that I was feeling like I was getting raped, but I didn't really know for sure.

The trip down was long and tiring, but for some reason the trip back was longer and humiliating, too. I had a race car, parts, an extra motor and a very excited little girl, but I could not shake the feeling I had just given away my dream hot rod for a pile of junk. I used his little car trailer to haul the race car back to Olympia and left my trailer with the seller as part of our transaction, something else that would haunt me later. I asked him how new his trailer tires were and he said "new." I asked about the wiring on the trailer, was it working? "Yes, perfectly," was the response.

On the trip back from central California, I had Jessica drive because I needed to close my eyes; part of this was fatigue from the long drive and the other part was stress over the deal I had just done. If we were going to make it to Roseburg, Oregon, that night I needed a little break. With all the confidence in the world, I had Jessica take the wheel of the full-size pick-up towing the race car on a little trailer headed north at the ripe old age of 15 with a learners permit.

Jessica did a perfect job behind the wheel towing the bright-yellow race car and dumpy little trailer. Four hours into our return trip, Jessica and I switched and an hour later we had nearly arrived in Weed, California, when we were hit by a severe thundershower that completely soaked the race car, spare engine and all the parts. I didn't know a lot about race cars, but I did know rain and rust would not be a good thing.

Temperatures all day had been in the high 80s but when dark clouds began to form the temperature dropped 25 degrees in five minutes and then the downpour started. Every part we had started rusting; our $35,000 TOE motor was soaked! Thankfully, just a couple hours later the temperature was back in the 80s and everything started to dry out at 65 mph. After the sun set it started to cool down but doing the math in my head I figured we would arrive in Roseburg by 11 that night.

Then we got another surprise: traveling at about 65 mph a trailer tire blew out. We were 11 miles from nowhere and, better yet, there was no spare tire. I could not believe this. We drove north on I-5 at 20 mph to the next small town, hoping to find a hotel and tire store. We found both and I told the girls to plan on being up early as we would need to get a tire and get back on the road to Olympia.

Once we got settled the girls wanted to have a little fun so they got the hotel manager to let them play in the pool even though it was very late; they needed to unwind from the stress of the tire situation we experienced for the last couple of hours.

I woke the girls at seven the next morning, started the truck and we idled over to the tire shop. One good look in daylight and I could tell this was going to get expensive. It was a wonder we didn't blow all four trailer tires because they were all rotted. Four brand-new trailer tires later and an hour spent fixing faulty wiring in the seller's trailer and we were on our way home.

A few weeks after our return from California to pick up our new race car, I reached out to a local and very well-respected crew chief, asking him to look at my equipment and tell me how I did. Beaming with pride and anxiety at the same time, I showed him the car, telling him the story about the Bristol chassis and the great motors, and I showed him the pile of great parts and, oh yes, all the extra tires.

This crew chief told me in a very nice way "You should try to get your Cobra back!"

Looking over the car he said it was junk. He pointed out unsafe work that had been done, including that the seller had put in an illegal fuel cell. The transmission had also been switched out and the crew chief said the previous owner had basically swapped out all the good stuff for junk.

But what about the motors, I asked. He looked at them and said the motor in the car was illegal and noted the valve covers had been replaced and the oilers were not plumbed. He added the builder of that engine was no longer in business. I said, "Okay what about the other motor, the TOE?" He told me the builder of that engine was awesome and he offered to call him to get the full story on that motor. A day later I learned the TOE motor was okay but it had quite a bit more than six races on it. In fact it was more like 36 races and it would cost $11,000-$13,000 to fix the motor.

The crew chief told me to get rid of the car and not to put my daughter in it. He said if the guy really had his daughter in the car he must not have liked her too much. I was crushed!

In the end I sold that turn-key car with the 700 hp motor for $11,000, and I had a bill for another $11,000 to fix the TOE motor. I ended up giving my Cobra and trailer away for free! My first endeavor in stock car racing cost me $60,000 and all I had to show for it was a broken motor, a bunch of worthless tires and parts that didn't fit the car I bought.

Unfortunately, my next very expensive lesson was just a mere few months later and it ended up costing our family another $60,000 from my prized guitar collection.

The respected crew chief had become my trusted advisor; we had become comfortable with each other and he assured me I could trust him and that his name in racing and business was gold. He promptly told me everyone in racing was crooked and because I was so new to the sport and didn't know anything, the only person I could trust was him.

A couple months later we agreed he would sell me his used, "rebuilt" car for $20,000. The car had no motor or transmission but he would do all the work on it and we would save so much money and I would have a basically brand-new race car for the season opener. He mentioned he had purchased $5,000 brakes for the car, which was already set up for a compression motor; what I was buying was a compression-motor roller chassis so I was getting a steal of a deal.

I learned later he too had taken out the good parts and compression-motor accessories and put in junk. When my wife and I questioned our "trusted advisor" and his wife about expenses and the purchase they told us we didn't buy the car despite a dozen or so emails saying we were buying the "roller." Instead, they explained to us what our deal meant: according to them we didn't buy what we thought we bought, rather we were providing money for them to spend as they saw fit.

They would ensure Jessica's car was safe and they would purchase the equipment and supplies we would need to race the 2011 season. They would buy and build a new race car and then decide which car Jessica would drive. When we learned of this position my wife and I nearly fainted; we could not leave their house fast enough. According to them we co-owned the new and the old cars and we were also required to fund racing for both cars; they did not put a dime of their own money in at this point.

So, another $60,000 or so later we realized we had just invested another pile of money with nothing to show for it except a 6-year-old race car worth maybe $10,000 while our "trusted advisor" had a brand new race car worth about $50,000 with the money coming from the sale of my private guitar collection to fund this part of our introduction to auto racing.

We should have figured this out a little earlier, but when our "trusted advisor" told us he needed more money we just tried to make sure he had it and we believed it was for Jessica's car and racing — we didn't know any better. He would often tell us if we wanted Jessica to have the best and to be safe we needed to buy the best, and he reminded us his services were in demand by dozens of race teams.

This relationship drained our family financially and emotionally, and took all the fun out of racing. It did not take long for us to realize our "trusted advisor" was with us only as long as we could bring money. After he and his wife sucked the life and money out of us we were the enemy and all those new parts we bought were not in our humble little car.

CHAPTER 27 — ISN'T THERE A BETTER WAY?

Although I firmly believed in my daughter and her potential for success as a race car driver, I needed to ease the financial strain on our family and the strain on me. I knew I was the weak link, I knew she would do so much better if she had a real "owner" and crew chief.

For a while I think Jessica believed her dream and our story would end at this point as we didn't have any more money or possessions to sell. Jessica was so mature and composed when we talked as a family and although she wouldn't say it out loud, I think she had been convinced by our "trusted advisor" we did not have a chance without him and his knowledge. I could see the disappointment in her eyes and I could hear it in her voice; this only made me more determined to try and find a solution.

Convinced others would be interested in becoming part of the amazing story and opportunity that Jessica represented, I began to think of ways to bring in outside funding through sponsorship. At the same time, I needed to figure out how to undo the damage done by our "trusted advisor." Jessica now believed not only that we were doomed, but that Dad could not do anything to support her or the team except provide money.

This was a truly low point and one I will never forget.

I began what I now affectionately call "dialing for dollars," but after getting nowhere with several dozen calls it occurred to me we had a good story but we did not have a good cause. We needed to have more than a request for money; we needed to revisit the business model of sponsorship in motorsports. Jessica and I talked and I asked her what she would do if she had to race for a cause. I explained to her on our budget there wouldn't be funds to race in every event; we would barely be able to race once a month and if the car got wrecked that would be another big challenge as I did not know anything about building or repairing race cars.

After some thought, Jessica asked me one day: "How can I race and help children?" That was a brilliant idea, I thought. I would reach out to any programs related to helping children and we would raise sponsor dollars while giving my little girl a chance to pursue her dreams. I made as many as 25 calls a day, trying to describe a relationship we could use to help non-profits raise money and fund our program. Many of the organizations we talked to were completely supportive of creating a platform for us to help them raise money, but each and every time the conversation turned to funds for our program the dialogue quickly lost energy.

At this point I began to reflect on several conversations I enjoyed when I had the honor of meeting a few times with a very powerful and well-known motorsports personality from the Pacific Northwest.

This man, who was very generous with his time, had spent several years in NASCAR. Rather than tell me about all the great things racing had to offer, he told me about the realities and asked me to consider them before putting Jessica into that environment. He met Jessica and could tell she was very close to her Mother and I, she was mature and composed, but also he could tell she had led a very sheltered life and was a tad naive.

He was uncomfortably direct with me and for that I continue to be grateful because he warned me about what to expect. Before giving me the unvarnished truth about big-time racing, he said the sport will break up families and it will break you financially. If I still wanted to move forward, he added, here are some of the realities:

> Just about any NASCAR race team would take a driver if they brought along enough money. It's all about the money, he said, and don't let anyone tell you anything different. As a talented young female racer, Jessica would be interesting but without money she could have all the talent in the world without ever getting the chance to drive. He noted a list of drivers in the NASCAR top three series today who but for the money their parents brought would be doing something besides racing.

> Our family would experience extreme stress and strain, and every relationship we developed to help Jessica may end up blowing up because we didn't have racing knowledge or a background in the sport. Others would take our money and leave us with nothing. I told

him about my experience buying the first race car and he could only shake his head in disgust. The sport is as crooked and corrupt as any seedy business you can think of, he said. When I told him about our experience with the second car he nearly choked on his coffee.

➢ Anyone offering to help will probably do so because they believe Jessica may help them with their own interests. This could be dangerous and we must be careful with her and her future. He cautioned me that everyone wanting to be part of this story will try to get control of Jessica and, to the extent we allow it, take control from us.

➢ Even after finding the right group/partner to race with as a team, it should be no surprise at all that the moment we run out of money or can't fund our side they dump us like a bad habit. He said leading up to that point I would be asked to buy new equipment, supplies and car parts but 90 percent of the time it would not make it into Jessica's car but would go in another team car. Boy did that turn out to be so true!

After meeting Jessica this wise man was more excited and positive about her chances, but he constantly reminded me the sport is cannibalistic. Of course Pam and I had already learned this all too painfully.

As the father of a 16-year-old girl who had led an idyllic and in some ways extraordinary life with extraordinary talent and potential, I was truly at a loss. I was prepared to give everything I had to provide her opportunities, wanting to believe deep down inside that I was doing the right thing. At the karting level as we began to enjoy more success, I put more and more pressure on Jessica to work harder, try harder and be her best as well as putting more pressure on myself to do better in the pits for her. Intuitively, I realized the more racing we did the higher the risk factor would be for her, me and our relationship.

At this moment in time none of us was having fun when it came to the stock car. Stress from the first two car purchases and the sour relationship with our "trusted advisor" was putting strains on us as a race team and also as parents. Hoping to avoid a train wreck, and feeling guilty for the first two missteps, I began trying harder and harder to control every aspect of the racing, on and off the track. I began to fear I was the only one who truly understood what was in Jessica's best interest and how to keep her safe; I was not able to trust anyone else.

This was a dark time for us and I was on the edge of shutting the program down; I think Pam and Jessica too were ready to give it up.

As the father of this exceptional little girl I struggled daily with how to tell her about my own demons and fears, and that the added stress of financial constraints may result in an opportunity lost for her. This change would mean she would lead an ordinary life and her dreams would remain just dreams because I could not figure this out. How can I take it all away? And if I take it away, who am I doing it for? Her or us, her parents?

These are the questions Pam and I dealt with and continue to live with every day although our vision has changed to some degree; we race with much more clarity now.

CHAPTER 28 — FIRST SUPER STOCK RACE; THIS IS NOT FUN

Meanwhile, our "trusted advisor" had us all set for the first race of the season. We had our 5-year-old chassis and old transmission, duct-taped fenders, bent door bars and oh yeah, heat-cracked brake rotors. Sure, we bought a new transmission but it ended up in another car, not ours. Yes, we thought we were going to have nearly perfect car for the season opener as part of our deal, but, I guess we were ready.

The night was very chilly and the stress on Pam and I was more than words can describe. The relationship with our "trusted advisor" was getting worse day by day, hour by hour, and on top of all that I had a severe bout of the flu.

Jessica was nervous and was trying to follow the advice of our "trusted advisor" by doing her best to ignore me. I was ill, had no voice and a very poor attitude, and should have stayed home according to my wife. Jessica was in awe of how much more work was involved in car preparation, safety and driver requirements, but she handled the pressure well.

The pressure she was not dealing with well came from me and my distrust of our "trusted advisor."

This was the first time I had to deal with turning over complete control and emotionally I was not ready. I wanted to believe our "trusted advisor" had Jessica's best interest at heart — later I learned he did not, but I also know he did not want anything bad to happen — but would he be able to get her to perform like I did? I didn't know for sure. Accordingly, I made a real ass of myself and said things reminiscent of the cruel and belligerent things my father said to me. It was a side of me Pam and Jessica rarely if ever saw, and it came out at the worst possible time.

When it was time to qualify, our "trusted advisor" remained cool and tried to keep Jessica focused. I was so irate, frustrated and scared all in one while trying to deal with the situation that I just tried to stay out of the way. After Jessica made her qualifying run and came into the pits she was looking for me to reassure her that we were okay and she was doing fine, but instead something remarkably stupid came out of my mouth. I don't have any idea of what I said but it was clear I had just killed her confidence and I had done it after she qualified eighth.

Flashbacks of racing with my dad began to haunt me and I suddenly felt like I was trying to destroy my daughter's dream. I knew better, I was better than that; I would not betray my little girl!

Just as I was about give up Pam acted quickly and with a great deal of diplomacy got control of the downward spiral that was taking place right in front of her. With rage in her eyes she said: "You are acting like your father. Stop it, stop it now or you are going to lose your little girl!" This wake-up call, delivered by Pam in the pits, hit me over the head and shook me like an earthquake.

I walked around to the front of the truck alone and asked myself the silly questions we all ask ourselves when trying to justify our stupidity or poor judgment, or better yet, when we try to rationalize our poor performance by asserting omnipotence. Try as I might, I was not having fun, I did not trust our "trusted advisor" and I was watching my little girl turn her back on me not out of fear but out of necessity. I had turned into the ugly monster I vowed to her, with tears running down my face when she was only an hour old, that she would never see.

The emotions this revelation raised caught me off guard and I stood there in front of the truck, fighting back tears. Something was not right, this was not fun and for the first time in our very short racing story I could not figure out how to fix it. For months I had been telling her at some point Dad would not be able to do it all and she would need to show me and the world she was the real deal. That night she was ready but when it came time for me to step up and do my part, I was not.

The smell of race gas hanging in the breeze, the dimly-lit pits, chilled spring air and sounds of racing snapped me back to reality — we had a race to run. Jessica talked to her crew and the "trusted advisor," discussing race strategy while I was sat in the trailer trying to remove myself just enough to be supportive and let be what was going to be. I gave my headset to Matt

Kindrick, who came along from Jessica's kart team, so he could talk to her and I went to watch the first of two 50-lap races from the bleachers.

That night Jessica took the green flag for her first Super Stock race. She was 16 and had completed less than 100 laps of practice in a full-size race car. Driving a 2,800-pound car into turns at 90-95 mph with 12 other cars on track was a lot for her to process, but I could see she was teaching herself car control, braking, throttle control and track awareness, giving it everything she had.

I had seen this before in karting, but her confidence was not that strong and then her spotter, the wife of our "trusted advisor," made the situation much worse with very poor communication and a lack of awareness. These two dynamics were visible on the track and I knew the situation would not get any better with the current team. We were not having fun; our "trusted advisor" saw Jessica as merely a little girl and possible resource he could direct for his own personal needs and with little regard for our family or finances.

Despite all that, Jessica drove a very smart race, made several clean passes and ended up with a solid top-five finish in her very first stock car race.

The second race of the evening was even more stressful, partly because I had set the tone of the evening with my poor judgment and poor attitude aggravated by flu. Jessica now had 50 laps of racing behind her and was moments from taking her second green flag for another 50-lap race. I walked down to the staging area where cars lined up before being called out on track, and found Jessica sitting in her car. I bent over close so she could hear me through her helmet and over the noise of the other cars, and said, "I love you, go have fun."

It was all she could do to say, "I love you back" and then she turned away to focus on the race about to be called up. I was devastated and felt powerless to do anything about it; our "trusted advisor" and his wife, as if it was their opportunity, began driving a wedge between me and my little girl once they sensed the dynamic between Jessica and I taking place that night.

Jessica took her second stock-car green flag and began to work her way through the field. Before long she was running fifth and gaining on the

142

leaders. This was amazing and for a moment I was not Daddy or crew chief, I was someone fascinated by what I was watching unfold. With just 10 laps to go Jessica was running in fourth place but she got a little wide coming out of turn 4 and brushed the wall, the impact putting her into a full-speed spin going into turn 1. She locked up the brakes and smoke rolled over the car from the burning rubber as she nearly hit the wall. It took her only a few seconds to restart the car and get back on track but she fell back to fifth. Undaunted, Jessica passed the fourth-place driver again and that was where she finished: fourth overall.

Jessica's superb performance — two top-five finishes in her first two races! — was over-shadowed by my less than stellar performance as a crew member and, more importantly, as a father. I needed to figure this out for me and for Jessica and most importantly for Pam. She was watching her family being torn apart and those thoughtful words of wisdom I heard earlier from someone who I value greatly began to resonate.

I called a family meeting a few days after her first race and, barely able to control my emotion, shared with Pam and Jessica that I was not comfortable with the current situation. It was no longer fun and we seemed to have lost the joy we once had. Jessica, Pam and I all struggled to keep our eyes dry and Jessica even said she would give up her dream if racing in the future was going to be anything like our first Super Stock race.

The next few weeks were spent regaining each other's trust and confidence and confirming there was still the passion to race. I needed to figure out a solution and Jessica needed to get comfortable with the increased responsibilities and danger of this new racing platform. After much soul-searching and a few more family meetings — of which Pam and Jessica would prefer we never have another — as a team and family we decided to end the relationship with our "trusted advisor" as a much needed first step to moving forward.

By making this decision we were about to learn just how much money we had lost in the relationship. After finding out all the money we had spent for Jessica to race had gone into another car, we were told there was another $15,000 of unpaid expenses we owed. If there was any doubt about us making the right decision this revelation made our decision perfectly clear. Some months later during a very candid conversation with a close friend of our "trusted advisor," I was told changing agreements or understandings, not doing promised work and creating overall hate and discontent was business as usual for this man and his wife. Several conversations with other race teams later confirmed the same.

After some discussion with Jessica, Mom and Matt, we decided to try racing the Super Stock without the experience or "help" of our "trusted advisor." Jessica and Pam struggled the most with this decision; mostly out of fear of going forward without the knowledge or experience we needed in the pits and for the car. The reality we faced at that point was that we no longer had the resources to race full-time. So we would race for fun and within the means we could generate on our own.

During the week leading up to Jessica's second Super Stock race I realized we were short a couple crew members; we did not have any race experience on the team and we did not have anyone who knew car set-up and tuning. We were as green as fresh-cut grass stuck to a lawnmower blade after mowing the lawn.

Out of just pure dumb luck we got a nice young guy named Brad Shaw to be our spotter because Matt, our "go to" guy, had a wedding to attend. I also picked up three more green guys to be the Jessica Dana Racing crew. Our driver was 16 with just two races to her credit, our crew was not sure what hole to put the gas in, and I had no idea at all how to make the car perform.

On paper this was a disaster looking for a place to happen. At a minimum, this was going to be a night to remember but this was also an experience and challenge Jessica and I were both eager and prepared to take on: we had been in this position many times before.

CHAPTER 29 — GOING IT ALONE, GETTING THE FUN BACK

When we arrived at the track for our second Super Stock event, I told the crew our first priority was the safety of our driver, the second priority was to have fun and enjoy the day, and the third and final priority I felt the urge to proclaim was to give it our all. Deep inside I was so nervous I thought I would toss my cookies at some point, but I needed to make sure neither the crew nor Jessica sensed it.

Jessica was calm and collected and was doing her best to hide her trepidation about her green crew. She was not all that sure of my ability to set-up the car and make adjustments, but she had made up her mind to carry me and her team if she had to. I had the same disposition; together we were a team.

Coming off the track from the first practice session Jessica was a little frustrated and she asked me if I was trying to kill her. She said it with a light-hearted giggle in her voice, but I got the hint that something was wrong with the set-up. The crew and I went back to work, made some changes, added back more air in the tires and then sent her back out for the second practice. The car was much better, Jessica said when she came back in, and the stopwatch agreed with her. Her 14.3-second lap was still slow compared to the fastest five cars but we were not too far off. Jessica's personal best lap at the track was 14.21, but that had come with our "trusted advisor" running the show. We knew there was no chance to get Jessica to that pace with our present team, but we kept trying to find more speed anyway.

Then the unexpected happened.

In the short period of time we'd been involved in stock car racing at the track Jessica had won the respect of several of her fellow racers and crewmembers from other teams, and out of nowhere those people came over and offered suggestions, grabbed tools and started helping. This inspired our crew to work even harder and by the end of practice Jessica laid down a 14.18 lap — a new personal best! Jessica and her crew celebrated as if we had just won the darn race; we were jubilant about performing for our driver, and our driver was thrilled about performing for her team.

I gathered the team for a quick talk and to a man and woman we agreed to try even harder to find more speed and prove to everyone Jessica was the real deal and that she and her team could compete with anyone on the track.

Next up was qualifying, two timed laps around the track to set the stating grid. The fastest car would start on pole, the second fastest completed the first row and so on. Our pride was on the line and we wanted to start better than the back of the field, so we made some last-minute changes to the car. With just a few minutes to go before the technical inspection and then qualifying, the team gathered around Jessica and gave her a round of high-fives. I was smiling from ear to ear: we had a team and we were there to race.

Jessica was the sixth car to qualify, and after getting on the track she ran the car through the gears and picked up her pace. Completing her first timed lap the stopwatch said 14.23 and we held our breath as she started the final lap. I watched the car intently through the circuit and felt good — the nose settled nicely into turn 3, she picked up the throttle perfectly in turn 4 — and when I looked up I saw 14.11, making her for the moment the fastest car and provisional pole-sitter. We jumped up and down like we won the race; there was so much joy coming over the radio from Jessica about that lap you would have thought we had just won the Daytona 500.

The next three cars to qualify had 150 hp more than we did so we knew it was unlikely Jessica would start on pole, but we had showed what our team and driver were capable of. Everyone, including the fans, knew the comparison between cars was not apples to apples. Our team qualified fourth and in the process beat several seasoned and qualified race car teams and drivers with more horsepower. We were having so much fun racing with no expectations, and we were quickly earning the respect of fans, racers and the track crew. I could not have been more proud but the experience was a little bittersweet: our "trusted advisor" had pitted next to us for the event.

That was just qualifying, however. Next up were two 50-lap races, with the first in just 10 minutes. The crew was as ready as ready could be, even though none of us had any idea of what we would be called to do. Brad Shaw, Travis Frasier, Dawson Morris and Daddy watched our young driver take the green flag.

Brad got on the radio and quickly moved Jessica to the inside lane while encouraging her to push hard to keep pace with the leaders. The caution flag came out for a car that spun and hit the wall, and Brad reminded Jessica to stay low on the restart: she did not have the horsepower of the other drivers so she needed to get a good start. Green again and Brad was trying not to show his excitement but he was impressed with his young driver and her consistency: "Jess you're doing great," "13.9! 13.9! 13.9!" "You are closing in on the leaders!" Jessica made two awesome passes and before we knew it we were in fourth place and advancing on the leaders.

And then it happened. In the blink of an eye concrete powder and white paint dust flew up from under the flagman tower: Jessica had hit the wall and damaged the car badly. Brad keyed the mic and told Jessica she was okay and to keep driving, but her return message was a curt: "Something is wrong!" Brad replied, "Jessica you are fine, get going!" She paused just a moment before getting back on the radio to tell us she was bringing the car in, something was wrong with it.

Brad told her to stay out just as Jessica turned onto pit lane and slowed the car to a safe pit speed. We ran as fast as we could to the pit because we had three caution laps to fix the car or Jessica would go a lap down and likely finish last. One glance and our hearts sank: two flat tires and two bent rims. Then like a jolt of soured milk in my mouth, Jessica keyed the mic and yelled: "Change my tires and get me back on the track!"

A pit stop? Change tires? Can we do this? Holy cow, what is a pit stop anyway?

And as if we actually knew what we were doing, we changed the right side tires, got her on the ground and back in the race still on the lead lap. We finished fourth overall and could have easily been third if not for the contact with the wall. We were gelling as a team and it was one of the most gratifying experiences in my life, and it was my little girl showing exceptional leadership skills and poise that got us moving.

With about an hour and a half to go before the final 50-lap race of the night, we had a lot of work ahead of us to try to get the car competitive again. We set the sway bar, added a spring rubber, made an air pressure change and went up on the track bar — this I learned by reading as much as I could off the Internet. We were not exactly sure what all that meant but we did it and then spent the next 45 minutes or so relaxing and re-living the most amazing night we were having. We set a team goal for the second race to finish with the car in one piece. We all got some food and caught our collective breath.

With the 10 minute to go call, we gathered up our driver, did a final check on air pressure and pushed the car to the staging line. Jessica was starting fourth which wasn't perfect but we were confident in her ability. Then a track official approached me to say they needed to move Jessica up a row to outside pole because the car in front of us failed inspection after the first race. Moving to the front row had Jessica terrified; a mistake made in front of the entire field could end up being more than just embarrassing, it often ended with taking the car home in pieces.

Never before in our racing had she needed me more to just stand by her while she waited for the race director to order engines to be started. We made small talk and Jessica said she was having trouble breathing but I tried not to make a big deal of it. She was nervous and feeling the pressure. I told her several times she would be fine and let her know I had spoken with the crew chief of the car behind us; he agreed his driver would give Jessica some time to get into the low grove or pass the pole sitter.

I knelt down next to the car and she extended her hand out to me. We held hands and Jessica squeezed my hand as if she was trying not to fall off a cliff. We made eye contact and both got tears in our eyes, we didn't need to say another word, we each knew what the other was thinking; this was special.

This was a moment we had discussed many times; this was a moment I will never forget.

It reminded me of another amazing race we had karting when we won even though on paper there was no way we should have, but we did. As I was

148

drifting back, recalling the conversation as we were driving home from PGP Motorsports Park that day, we talked about the things we used to do together and her memories and thoughts about what we have done together. I told Jessica with my emotions barely in check that I would gladly trade the last 10 years of my life for one year with her when she was 5 years old. Jessica asked why I picked 5, but then she paused and said, "I know, 5 was when I started riding and me and you would go to the dunes all the time and camp and play." I replied, "No, Hun, 5 was when I realized I was the luckiest Dad on earth."

With the minute to go before the notice to fire engines we held hands, she would not let go. I did one last radio check and walked around the car to satisfy myself she would be okay, and with that it was all business. Fans, ignition, wham! The motor blasted to life and she was rolling out to the track for driver introductions. After that the crowd helped give the command to start engines and Brad and I took turns talking to Jessica to prepare her for starting on the outside pole; I was a nervous wreck!

Suddenly, race control directed Brad to move Jessica to the back of the field; we were being penalized for taking two new tires after the wall contact in the first race. Apparently our "trusted advisor" complained to race officials we had taken two new tires when according to him we needed only one. This from a man who had been racing his entire life and whose car had 150 hp more than ours and was the fastest on the track! This petty disposition would haunt us all summer. We tried hard to get Jessica to understand why she was being moved to the back but even though she complied, she did not get it. We did not tell her then it was because of him.

The green flag went up and Brad keyed the mic, yelling: "Green! Green! Green!" After just a few laps we could tell this race was going to be wild.

Cars in front of us were beating and banging and then the first caution flag came out. Two drivers were penalized for aggressive racing and moved to the back. A few more laps and a crash, a few more laps and more aggressive driving penalties, and before we knew it we were in third! Another caution flag came out for another spin out and we were in second place! A few minutes later after another caution we were in first place with 10 laps to go.

Brad and I talked to Jessica during the caution laps, explaining to her how to get the best start with all the high horsepower motors behind us.

Green! Green! Green! It was a drag race into to turn 1 and we lost, but Jessica moved comfortably into second place with five laps to go. She was driving amazing but suddenly when the white flag came out a slower car dropped oil on the track, causing a crash when another car hit the slick spot. We got Jessica under the oil in turns 1 and 2 but the yellow did not come out so Brad yelled "Go go go!" But entering turn 3 Jessica hit oil from the same slow car and spun backwards into the wall. Not losing her composure she got the car rolling and crossed the finish line in fourth place.

The emotional rollercoaster took a toll on the couple hundred people who were there cheering for Jessica but it took even more out of Pam and I! Jessica rolled into the pit stall dejected but proud of what she did and about 200 people showed up to sign the hood of her car after the race. The crew all came together and we agreed that had almost been a storybook ending. Then I looked over the rear of the car at Travis and Brad and told them it would be a storybook ending if it ended all today and she thinks we're just racing!

CHAPTER 30 — MONEY STRUGGLES; THE RIGHT CREW CHIEF

Pam, Jessica and I had a discussion and came to the agreement we did not enjoy the way things were working. Our former "trusted advisor," fueled by vitriolic hate and discontent from his wife, who was often referred to by other drivers as the toughest man in the pits, made racing uncomfortable on and off the track. That, as well as our lack of experience and diminishing confidence in Brad, who we liked just fine but deep down I knew he did not have the right demeanor for our team. Brad was wired to be on 'kill mode' at all times whether he had a driver on the track or not.

With all this, my very conservative approach and not nearly enough money to fix things properly, I figured it would only be a matter of time before our team lost its energy and the journey ended.

Rather than try and make the next race in a couple of weeks, Jessica and I decided to take a break from the race track and go to the sand dunes to just reconnect. We rode quads for three days, did not mention race cars or racing and just enjoyed being together at the dunes — something we had done dozens and dozens of times before.

Waiting for us back at home was a bent-up race car, a media firm wanting Jessica to sign an exclusive marketing, brand and professional services agreement, and a TV show deal about our journey with a 10-year commitment.

And we no longer had the funds to race.

At this point I had already sold my guitar collection and those funds ended up in the new race car of our "trusted advisor." Jessica was much better than the talent I had been able to put around her on and off track, and I needed to fix that if we were going to race. Bottom line was I needed to make some changes if we were going to do what we had in the past: have fun and run towards the front of the pack.

I heard from a friend of a friend that Neil Derline, a crew chief with 20 years of experience including working 11 years with local late-model legend

Tom Sweatman, would not be working with Tom in 2011 on asphalt but would be helping him on the dirt track in Elma, Washington.

I decided to call Neil to introduce myself and our team. After explaining to him we were a very green crew with a 16-year-old rookie driver, who by the way was a girl, Neil agreed to come to our shop to look at our car and meet our team. He made it clear he was not available to crew very much due to his continuing relationship with Tom Sweatman, who was making a change from asphalt to dirt-track racing. I suspected he was a little curious and bored with dirt racing, or maybe just wanted to see what the buzz was about as I later learned he had heard in the rumor mill there was a 16-year-old girl turning some heads at the speedway.

After several positive phone conversations with Neil, he met with our team one afternoon at our humble little race shop. Brad, Matt, Jessica, and Mom and Dad were anxious to meet the legend who helped Tom Sweatman win hundreds of races. Besides being admired and respected in the local racing community, Tom had an opportunity to race for a NASCAR Cup series team in the late 1990s.

Neil pulled up to the shop in a white 1987 Ford Mustang that sounded very healthy for a little pony car, and he climbed out of the car slowly. Neil had a kind smile and lean build and was about 6-foot tall when standing erect, a position he is rarely in as his back was permanently injured in a logging-truck accident six years ago. The damage to his back is so severe walking bent over at the waist is the most comfortable way for him; if he stands straight up he can walk only short distances.

After introductions Neil looked over the race car and noted that it was a clean car, it looked well cared for and he asked if this was the car we got from our "trusted advisor." When I told him it was and how much we paid, he was shocked and said we had been taken advantage of. Neil crawled under the car, asking many questions: Do you have a spare motor or transmission? Answer: No. Do you have any scales? No. Do you have any spare parts? No. Do you have any spare shocks or springs? No.

After about five more questions Neil got the picture: we had a car, four wheels and a few tools. We all sat around a little table eating pizza and discussing what had happened to that point, where we were and where we wanted to go. Neil looked Jessica right in the eye and asked her what it was she wanted or expected. Jessica said to have fun, feel safe and win!

Neil finished our two-hour get-to-know-each-other-over-pizza meeting by agreeing to go to the next race with us and help on the car. But, he added, he would not be available to make every race or work much on the car between races. As a team we looked at each other and smiled with relief; at least we would have a little help from a proven crew chief. To a man and women the team liked Neil and hoped he would enjoy working with us.

A few days before the first race Neil would help us with, he came to the shop and spent several hours poring over and under the car, looking at every nut, bolt, screw and other part. He came back the next day — a 45-minute drive each way — with a carload of spare parts, tools and scales he said we could use if needed. Neil added he would meet us at the track for our first race as a team.

It was an unusually cool summer night and Neil, Matt, Travis, Brad, Jess and I were going to give it a go as Jessica Dana Racing: JDR. Dozens of drivers and crewmembers from other teams recognized Neil and stopped by our pit to ask him how he was doing and why the heck he was crewing for a 16-year-old girl. Always pleasant and never saying a bad word about anyone, Neil would just smile and say he was going to give us a little help and see what happened.

From my perspective, Neil's impact was positive and instantaneous, but the rest of the team was not entirely sold, including Jessica. My role expanded to interpreter and mediator, helping Jessica and Neil communicate, which was difficult for both, and keeping the team and Brad focused on their new roles and responsibilities. Jessica's past experiences with tuners and crew chiefs made her a little skeptical. In the past Neil always had an experienced driver who knew what he wanted and needed, but now he had a teenage girl who had no idea how to communicate what she wanted or needed due to lack of experience.

By all accounts our first race with Neil was a success with a top-five finish and I could sense Neil was impressed with Jessica, but also that he realized our team was a completely different environment than he was used to. I also came to realize Brad would not likely be on the team for our next race as he crossed the line with Jessica in the pits after the end of the race, yelling at her for not driving harder.

At a post-race team meeting it was confirmed we would go forward without Brad, and we would try to add another female to the team in addition to replacing Brad as spotter. Visibility is limited in a low-slung and fast moving race car, making the spotter a critical member of the team as he or she is the driver's mirror and strategist. With a 16-year-old girl with little race experience at the wheel, I knew how difficult a job it would be. Having spotted for Jessica in karts I felt as if I could do it, but Jessica and I both preferred finding a quality spotter before our next race; I did not like being spotter and my lack of experience would be a liability for her on the track.

If these challenges were not enough we were beginning to attract serious interest in JDR and a possible TV show, and I was still pursuing possible sponsorship opportunities by making countless calls day-in and day-out; we needed more money to fund the racing.

The car was still intact except for a few bent bars, so after some sticker repair work, light welding and a little extra duct tape, we were ready for the second race with Neil. We had no luck getting a new spotter after Jessica let Brad know we would be looking for other options at that position, but we added Mary Ann Bringhurst, a stunning 5-foot-9 college volleyball player with a passion for competition and a desire to play a role on a team.

Dad was going to take the spotter duties and not a person on the JDR team felt good about it, including me! Jessica made it clear by her demeanor that she would not tolerant or accept mistakes based on my lack of experience as a spotter.

Neil and the team were as ready as we could be for our second race together and qualifying proved it as we recorded our best qualifying time of the season with a 14.09-second lap. The first of two 50-lap races started with Jessica running confidently in third place and laying down fast laps. I was trying my hardest to figure out how to be a spotter and not confuse her while she continued to turn low 14-second laps.

Somewhere around lap 15 or 20, way too early to be getting impatient, a faster car caught up to her rear bumper. The driver made a single attempt to pass her on the outside but realizing he could not get around that way he dove to the inside. Just as he made his move I keyed the mic and said, "Inside" as a way of telling Jessica to move up the track and let him by, but I was not quick enough and he drove straight into her door. Jessica was hit so hard her car lifted two or three feet off the ground and spun into the wall in turn 2. I keyed the mic and asked if Jessica was okay. She said she was fine and she was upset, very upset: that crash was not her fault. She was right; it was a combination of her spotter and a bonehead driver in a red car.

The team worked franticly for about two hours trying to repair the car for the second 50-lap race of the night. Pulling me off to the side, Neil told me the car frame was badly twisted; the rear end was not square to the frame. He said the car would be safe to race but it would not be safe for much more than 50 or 60 laps. How he could tell that I had no clue. Neil pointed to the damaged area and said he compensated for the twisted frame by resetting the rear end; the car would not be perfect but Jessica could run in the back and earn points.

I got my courage up to spot again but with a high degree of anxiety knowing the car was wrong and that I needed to find a way to keep Jessica racing and not scare her. I asked way too many questions and she became very impatient, but it was what we had to do. The second race went well and, twisted car and all, Jessica and I managed to make a couple of passes and finish without further damaging the car.

When we tore the car down after the race and saw just how badly it was damaged, we knew making the next race was out of the question. That meant the end of Jessica's chance at earning rookie of the year honors. When it was all said and done we had more than $2,500 in damage and that would be with our team doing most of the repair work.

CHAPTER 31 — MAKING HISTORY AT THE MILLER 200

It was beginning to become clear Neil was having a lot of fun with us, and in turn we were starting to have fun with him. On Sunday afternoon after the race while Pam, Jessica and I were recovering from the night before, Neil called to say he was on his way. He just could not stand not knowing for sure what needed to be fixed. After a couple hours working on the car, Pam cooked dinner and we sat around with our stomachs full talking about our next race, the Miller 200. We were becoming excited and confident again, thinking maybe we could do this and maybe we just might have the makings of a young race team after all. Neil by contrast was very apprehensive about putting Jessica in with the wolves.

The team opted to sit out the race before the Miller 200 to save the car and direct our resources to the Miller, the year's largest and most prestigious race at South Sound Speedway. The final field was expected to be more than 30 drivers, including many of the biggest names in regional late-model racing.

On top of that, if Jessica made it into the starting field, she would make history as the youngest female to ever race in the Miller 200. Every other day Jessica and Mary Ann, with help from Aunty Kim, went out knocking on doors to look for sponsors and to their credit they landed $500 here and $500 there and that, along with the help of an anonymous donor, truly funded our participation in the Miller 200.

Because so many teams show up for a race like the Miller 200, the field for the A Main, the feature event, would be set by a two-step process. Eighteen of the 25 A Main starting positions would be set by qualifying, with the balance filled out by the top four finishers in the B Main — known as "racing your way into the show" — and two more selected as "promoter's provisionals." In the end 35 or 36 cars showed up to vie for the 27 starting positions in the A Main, but we felt even though the Miller 200 would be just her 10th career late-model race, fifth race night, Jessica could qualify on time and jump directly into the A Main.

In practice Jessica turned a 13.9-second lap but she was consistently in the 14.1 range. Unfortunately, Neil and I opted to make a few minor changes for qualifying, over Jessica's objections I might add, that did not have the desired effect and she ended up recording a lap of 14.2 that was only good enough for the seventh-place starting position in the B Main. For comparison, veteran racer Ron Eaton won the pole with a new track record lap of 13.41. I could feel the entire team's disappointment and concern after qualifying because we had done such a great job in practice, but everyone pulled together and determined we would just have to take a little longer path to the feature.

Jessica started the 15-lap B Main in seventh place but she clearly had one of the faster cars. Four laps after the green flag she had advanced two positions when the yellow flag came out for a crash. Clean-up took some time so the B Main was shortened to 10 laps. Jessica continued her strong run after the restart to finish third — racing her way into the Miller 200 and making history as the youngest female racer to start the race!

This effort did not go unnoticed by her fellow drivers and we were thankful so many of them, including JJ Hamilton, made an effort to help us and coach Jessica about the race and what to expect before the A Main. This was starting to feel like the culture and karting environment we enjoyed so much, and it was clear she was earning the respect of her fellow drivers.

Driving smart and staying out of trouble, Jessica steadily moved forward after starting the 200-lap A Main 23rd of 25 cars. She was inside the top-20 by the midpoint break and after getting two tires, fuel and a minor track-bar adjustment, Jessica continued to advance over the final distance of the race to finish 11th. "This was just as good as a win," said Neil after the race and I agreed with him entirely.

What I witnessed in addition to a pair of incredible drives by Jessica was a race team gelling around a driver who improved light years in one night. I was proud beyond words at what Jessica accomplished, racing her way into the Miller 200 and then nearly earning a top-10! And she thought we're just racing!

After the Miller 200 Neil was fully convinced Jessica was the real deal and almost overnight he became a selfless contributor to the team in every way. Jessica's dream had become his dream and his dream became part of the fabric of the team's dream.

The seasonal finale, September 10, 2011, at South Sound Speedway was bittersweet. Jessica clearly had become one of the fastest crate-motor drivers on track, consistently running in the front of the pack, and our JDR pit team was improving each and every time we arrived at the track. I was even getting better at spotting, although from the onset we had planned on finding a spotter with track experience and car knowledge for Jessica.

I had always figured we would make the change when the right guy came along and the day before the season finale I found the "right" guy and he was eager to spot for Jessica. When I mentioned it to her she said, calmly and firmly, "Daddy, you're the spotter." I tried to get support for the change from Neil, Matt and Travis, but no go! They all said not a chance, "You're the spotter." I went back to Neil a few minutes later and tried to sell him on getting Jessica a good spotter, but Neil said "You're doing fine, grab the radio and stop being a sissy."

Jessica once again proved she was the real deal laying down a 13.94 qualifying lap that put her starting sixth of the 21-car field for the first 50-lap race. With nothing to run for other than pride and after a little drama between the pole sitter and outside pole sitter, Jessica drove a very smart race and finished fifth with the car still in one piece.

Neil and I, along with the rest of the team, were having a blast; our young driver was fast and doing an incredible job behind the wheel. Jessica was having so much fun and her smile in and out of the car was a strong indication of how much she enjoyed the experience. The fifth-place finish set the grid for the season's last race and, after a couple of cars ahead of her opted to start in the back to avoid what was largely predicted to be a crash-fest, Jessica ended up starting third behind 2011 track champion Bob Pressley

I was gaining confidence with spotting and my driver, and by the last race Jessica and her team were all on the same page. We were going for it — we were going to try to win this race. "Green, Green, Green," I blurted into the mic as the flag dropped for the last race of the year. "Stay on him! Stay on him!" I spit into the mic as Jessica got a great run and cleared fourth place and moved into second.

Now in control and running strong behind the leader, Bob Pressley, Jessica started to run him down. I gave Jessica the "clear, clear, clear" message so she knew no other cars were on her and she began to close the gap with first place. My hands were trembling as I struggled to keep the excitement out of my voice and not make it obvious to Jessica; she needed to stay calm and I needed to stay calm!

Lap after Lap Jessica was driving like a machine and slowly she inched up and got under Bob and then everything changed — a caution flag for a spin in turn 4 on lap 20. Caution flags were our Achilles Heel as our little crate motor just didn't have the horsepower — or as Neil would often say "snort" — to pull with the big motors on a restart. Jessica had by now become one of the fan favorites and it showed as even the announcer knew the restart was not going to be good for us and mentioned over the public address that things might get a little crazy when the race went back to green.

We needed a good restart and we needed Jessica to hold position, but just a second after I blurted "green, green, green" it was clear we were going to lose several spots; we slipped back to fifth or sixth before she got back in the lower groove. Jessica was upset and it was my job to calm her down and keep her focused. Later, Neil and I learned the reason she got beat so bad was when all strapped in she could not reach the shifter well enough to shift up to third gear to help acceleration; Neil had a new shifter the next day but that didn't help us at the moment.

Getting focused again, Jessica started to close in on fifth place and she was obviously faster. Because she was clearly turning better than the other car, when she was a foot off his bumper I had her look first for an outside pass. Making a brilliant race move, she got to the inside of the other car coming out of turn 2 headed into turn 3. I yelled "outside, outside," and in the blink of an eye the other car turned down to cut her off entering turn 3, hitting Jessica's car at about 95 miles per hour. The impact shot her into the infield, out of control and headed for the wall, and every spectator and spotter knew this was going to be horrible wreck. Sliding sideways, throwing

159

gravel and dirt, Jessica hit the rumble strip and re-entered the track far too fast to stop before hitting the wall.

Then, as if she was an experienced drifter, Jessica stabbed the throttle and put the car into a four-wheel slide to avoid hitting the high wall between turns 3 and 4. She somehow managed to get the car headed right out of turn 4 but it was pointed at the exit wall. Then she did it again, tapping the brake and stabbing the throttle to whip the car violently to the left so the right rear quarter panel of the car just brushed the wall. Now the car was completely sideways going down the straightaway, but Jessica corrected it again and at the start-finish line she finally straightened out as the announcer screamed into the public address system: "What a save!"

The track was a mess and Jessica knew she had just avoided a major wreck. My hands were shaking all over the place as she asked me how I liked her save, adding a little giggle for emphasis. Neil got on the radio and said, "That was amazing!" All the cars were stopped on the track for the clean-up when a race official came up and told me to have Jessica pull into the pits: she was leaking oil and bad!

The impact tore a hole in the oil pan and there was no chance we would be able to get back on the track; we were done. Our night was over but our team was all smiles: yes, we wouldn't finish the race and yes, we got wrecked but, wow, what a night! Not a person on the team was down or upset; of course there was a lot of disappointment for what could have been, but what a drive and what night.

A few minutes later the driver of the other car came into our pit and apologized over and over. He said Jessica had the pass and the lane, and he just made a bonehead maneuver and we got wrecked because of it. Jessica was sure to let him know she races like she is raced. He got the hint!

Conclusion — what's next?

When I look at Jessica I still see my little girl who wanted to be tickled every day, who wanted her Daddy to fall asleep with her every night until she turned 13, and even occasionally after. Racing was never planned and we never dreamed or aspired to find ourselves in this position, but now the opportunity we created by accident is tantalizingly close — but also so remarkably far away.

The reality, that what we are doing is so much more than just racing, is inspiring. The transition from having my little girl relentlessly pursue me for our next great adventure, our next great challenge, our next great race, to now growing away from me in search of her own adventures and challenges away from the track has been difficult to say the least. I am however blessed at the track that I am still part of this story — or at least until she replaces me with a good spotter.

The next chapter is yet to be told and most likely will be written by Jessica herself. Her mother and I will always have a little girl who by all accounts could be the next great female race car driver or maybe the next great driver in motorsports period. The stress on the family, our finances and priorities make the sport of racing remarkably difficult to pursue, but the reward we get from the positive impact Jessica has on nearly everyone she touches with her drive and determination is limitless.

As a family of modest means and without the aid of sponsorship, our story may end like so many others with a return to more affordable sporting events like karting for fun. For this Dad and his little girl, that would provide the opportunity to recapture the innocence and joy we shared early in our introduction to motorsports.

We as a family do not know nor do we have any idea what lies ahead of us and for Jessica; time will only tell. What I do know vividly is the joy I got from holding her in my arms, the smell of her hair after a bath when she was just few days old, the content feeling I had when she would fall asleep on my chest at night, the excitement I had to see her every day when I got home from work and how she would run straight into my arms every day.

We would "westle" at night until my arms were noodles, we would spend days in the mountains just being together, making snacks, watching elk and deer. I would put her in the seat with me and let her drive the logging roads in the Cascade Mountains when she was only 5. At the only home she has known since she was born, we would work around the place, plant trees and gardens and watch them grow. I would often work in the wood shop until late at night building furniture for her and the house, and she would come out and tell me — with little hands on hips and just a tad sassy — "Daddy, it's time to come to bed! Now!"

I remember the first day she rode her ATV like it was yesterday; she barely had the strength to control the machine but she had the will, desire and drive in her DNA. She would ride with me for hours until her tiny thumb would get too sore from the throttle. She just loved going fast with both of us on my ATV doing high-speed laps on the little oval in our back yard, and I would wear out long before her.

I was never going to leave her behind or leave her out because she was a girl; I was not going to let her feel scared or alone; and I never wanted to take away from her the joy she had with me riding, racing or playing. On the other hand, I never wanted her to have the bad experiences I did racing with my Dad when he was at his worst. In an unexpected and amazing turnaround she is now the one leading her team and letting them know they won't be left behind. What is extraordinary is she has no intention of leaving me behind.

Our story is full of many amazing and wonderful experiences together as a family, more then we can remember if we tried, and thankfully very few undignified experiences. Motorsports, however, in some odd way has been something Jessica and I shared together and yet alone. Each of us has grown and learned from this experience. We are still remarkably close and each strives to make the other stronger, both on and off the track. We were the most unlikely team anyone expected to be competitive when we showed up at the track, we were always the least experienced, with modest resources and most humble equipment, yet it was me and my little girl doing the

162

unexpected, winning when we shouldn't, always the underdog.

I would guess Jessica will write the next chapter of this story after she has her own children and maybe, just maybe it will start with: "Just a little girl and her Daddy, doing what no one thought could be possible, and he thought we were just racing."

Daddy loves you, Princess!

SPECIAL THANKS

To Team JDR:

    Neil Derline (Crew Chief)

    Travis Frazier (Jackman)

    MaryAnn Bringhurst (Tires)

    Scott Haverlock (Body & Paint)

    Bryan Rolland (Car Chief)

    Kim Haverlock (Team Baker)

Pints and Quarts Pub, PintsAndQuartsPub.com

Scott Whitmore, 40 West Media, 40West.Wordpress.com

Lacey Casciato, sponsor relations

South Sound Speedway, Nick Behn, SouthSoundSpeedway.com

Knight Fire, Randy Knighton, KnightFire.net

First Citizens Bank, Vicki Churchill, FirstCitizensBank.com

TOE, Tony Oddo Jr., TOEperf.com

Ewing Race Engines, Elma, Washington: Dick Ewing

Pardiman Productions, Cory Pardiman, PardimanProductions.com

Vital Signs, Tacoma, Washington

VDL, Charlotte, North Carolina, Dan VanderLey, VDLFuelSystems.com

Wilbur Bruce, graphics

Greg Tranum, vice president of Print Northwest

Eddie Harris, artist

Budd Bay Café and Rivers Edge, Dannielle and Patrick Knutson, BuddBayCafe.com and RiversEdgeTumwater.com

Sam Thomassen, advisor

94.5 ROXY, Jerry Farmer, 945Roxy.com

John Lathrop Jr., he and his family are the best

JJ Hamilton

Jared and Kelly Vorse

Interested in becoming a sponsor and helping Jessica attain her racing dreams? Contact Troy Dana at Troy.Dana@d3rec.com.

Made in the USA
Charleston, SC
11 April 2012